Anti-Museum

Anti-Museum charts the development of the anti-museum as a concept and as it has been realised in practice. Drawing on a range of case studies, including the New Museum and PS1 in New York, Mona in Australia, Art42 in Paris and Donald Judd's Marfa, the book assesses their potential to engage museum publics in new ways.

Anti-museums seek to breathe relational and theatricalised vitality into the objects they exhibit, by connecting them to the contexts of their making, to their social life outside the museum, to visitors' lives via their transformative capacities for change, and by being a place of dialogue, exchange and transformation, rather than instruction. Documenting the ways in which they have been created by artists, collectors, and curators, the book also examines the extent to which anti-museums connect with other museums through the exchange of values and resources. Critically, it asks whether, after some 40 years of 'new museology', such institutions are still able to offer something fresh and valuable.

Anti-Museum provides a sharp and incisive account of the anti-museum as it has been imagined, realised and experienced, and as it has relevance for understanding and working in the contemporary museum world. As such, the book will be of great interest to scholars and students engaged in the study of museums, cultural economy, inclusive urban regeneration, the democratisation of art and contemporary art. It should also appeal to museum professionals around the world.

Adrian Franklin is Professor of Creative Industries and Cultural Policy at the University of South Australia.

Museums in Focus
Series Editor: Kylie Message
Australian National University, Australia

Committed to the articulation of big, even risky ideas, in small format publications, 'Museums in Focus' challenges authors and readers to experiment with, innovate, and press museums and the intellectual frameworks through which we view these. It offers a platform for approaches that radically rethink the relationships between cultural and intellectual dissent and crisis and debates about museums, politics and the broader public sphere.

'Museums in Focus' is motivated by the intellectual hypothesis that museums are not innately 'useful', safe' or even 'public' places, and that recalibrating our thinking about them might benefit from adopting a more radical and oppositional form of logic and approach. Examining this problem requires a level of comfort with (or at least tolerance of) the idea of crisis, dissent, protest and radical thinking, and authors might benefit from considering how cultural and intellectual crisis, regeneration and anxiety have been dealt with in other disciplines and contexts.

Anti-Museum
Adrian Franklin

Queering the Museum
Nikki Sullivan and Craig Middleton

www.routledge.com/Museums-in-Focus/book-series/MIF

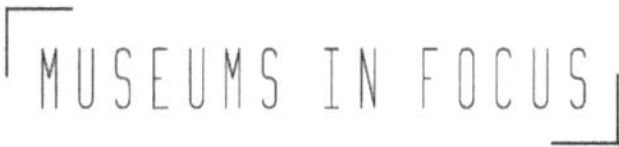

Logo by James Verdon (2017)

Anti-Museum

Adrian Franklin

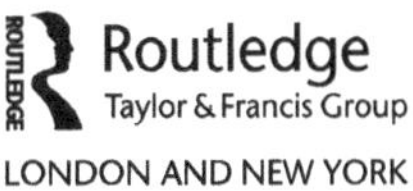

LONDON AND NEW YORK

First published 2020
by Routledge
2 Park Square, Milton Park, Abingdon, Oxon OX14 4RN

and by Routledge
52 Vanderbilt Avenue, New York, NY 10017

Routledge is an imprint of the Taylor & Francis Group, an informa business

First issued in paperback 2021

British Library Cataloguing-in-Publication Data
A catalogue record for this book is available from the British Library

Library of Congress Cataloging-in-Publication Data
A catalog record has been requested for this book

ISBN: 978-1-138-60412-4 (hbk)
ISBN: 978-1-03-208668-2 (pbk)
ISBN: 978-0-429-46867-4 (ebk)

Typeset in Times New Roman
by Wearset Ltd, Boldon, Tyne and Wear

For Lynn

Contents

Figures

Acknowledgements

Thanks are due to Chris McAuliffe for suggesting that I write something for Kylie Message's *Museums in Focus* series, perhaps something on Mona to follow up her own book *The Disobedient Museum*. It was a great opportunity to focus on Mona's activism but there was an even greater opportunity to situate Mona's activism among the activisms of other self-styles anti-museums. I would like to thank Kylie Message and Heidi Lowther for their wisdom, support and encouragement with this idea and helping me turn it into a book. Many others have provided their time and resources to make it possible, they include: Karen Wong, Sarah Lombardi, David Walsh, Olivier Varenne, Mark Fraser, Jean-Hubert Martin, Leigh Carmichael, Elizabeth Pearce, Terry Smith, Nicolas Laugero Lassserre, James Brett, Sergio, Judd Foundation, Chinati Foundation, Juliette Cléraux, Paul Jackson, Jacqui Woolf, Emma Whelan, Jennifer Lees, David Keller, Arlette Martin, Amye McCarther, Vincent Monod, Andrea Walsh, Sadie Coles, Natalie Oleksy-Piekarski, Isabelle Bezzi, Debbie Hillyerd, Katerina Bryant, Marc Stratton, Denise Meredyth, Jason Bainbridge, Liz Nowell, Julie White and Craig Hicks. Special thanks are due to Kangan Gupta at Routledge.

1 Introduction

Anti-museum – imagining the unthinkable

This book opens up a new line of enquiry into a leading edge of experimentation and innovation in museum design and practice that was championed by anti-museums. As the name suggests, anti-museums deliberately opposed and reversed the founding principles and aims of what Bennett (1995) calls 'the modern museum', and, in most cases they are anti-museums of art. The book will establish their origins, what they do and why, what they have in common (and yet why they are also so diverse), and what impact they have had on visitation, museology and the development of art and art publics.

These 'outsider institutions' have been steadily growing in number and reputation since the 1940s, though such are the myriad ways in which convention can be opposed that they never formed a stable binary opposite, or a 'successor to', the modern museum in any formal, or collective sense. Nor did they wish to, standardisation was one of the things they opposed. Certainly, no attempt was made to form a new museological movement or art movement. Their strength is expressed instead through their individuality, through their flexibility and capacity to respond intimately to the art worlds around them – which are always particular and ecological (if not exclusively 'local') – and through a studied avoidance of collective manifestos, credos, directives or external control. They were almost all experimental, artist-, rather than art history-focussed and interested in developing active new roles in the production and development of art, in its curation and exhibition and more appropriate forms of dissemination to wider audiences. They had pedagogical ambitions but avoided didacticism. After a consideration of their conceptual and historical evolution in this chapter, the book will focus on six detailed case studies of anti-museums in the USA, Europe and Australia.

To many people, the idea of opposing museums, let alone building anything called an anti-museum, might seem absurd: such is the respect accorded them as centres of learning, and such is the fondness with which they are recalled from childhood visits and pleasurable associations with leisure, holidays and tourism. Art museums and galleries are treasured pillars of modern civilisation; they are woven into the fabric of contemporary life and we are currently in the middle of a renewed museum building phase globally. Much hope is pinned to their capacity to catalyse cultural and economic regeneration and most, if not all, of this growth is in the conventional public museum sector. It is true they are loved, but they loved most by a minority dominated by sections of the educated elite. Indifference or ambivalence to them is prevalent in other social groups (Prior 2002; Green 2018; Franklin and Papastergiadis 2017).

It is rare to find more than a quarter of the adult population in any nation having visited an art museum in the previous 12 months. While rates for children are higher, at around 40 per cent, this is largely the result of art museum-going in school curricula. Art museum-going as a life-long pursuit, however, is largely confined to sections of the tertiary educated middle classes, and given that art museums were widely founded in the nineteenth century precisely to encourage *everyone* to enjoy the benefits of art, and not just the social elite (who collected art and displayed it in their homes), the modern art museum project might be judged a failure on its own terms. These were among the reasons why art critic John Berger was very far from impressed by them. In 1969, he also wrote that art museums were 'inadequate and outdated'; their curators were 'patronising, snobbish and lazy'. Further, Berger fumed about a view, common within art museum circles, that the pleasure of art derived from 'well-formed taste' and that 'appreciation' derived from 'connoisseurship'. For Berger, both views were 'mired in eighteenth century thinking', just as their treatment of the working class as 'passive [and] made to feel like paupers receiving charity and instruction', belonged to the nineteenth century (Berger 2018, pp. 171–172; see also Leahy 2010, pp. 162–163).

Views such as these were common enough around the mid-twentieth century, and they prompted a new wave of frustration with the conventional art museum, that emerged especially within the contemporary art movements of the 1950s and 1960s. These were aided and abetted by the alternative society movements, civil rights and liberation politics of the post-war period. Under the pressure to rebuild, democratise and modernise, there were renewed calls for art to be more diverse, contemporary and future-facing. The Institute of Contemporary Arts in London, founded in 1947, was a path-breaker in this respect. While it deliberately decided not to be a museum, it went further than this by organising its programme in ways that actively opposed the culture of art museums. Critical reviews of its early years jubilantly described it as an anti-museum (e.g. Cranfield 2014). Also from the late 1940s, a circle of Paris-based artists around Jean Dubuffet became

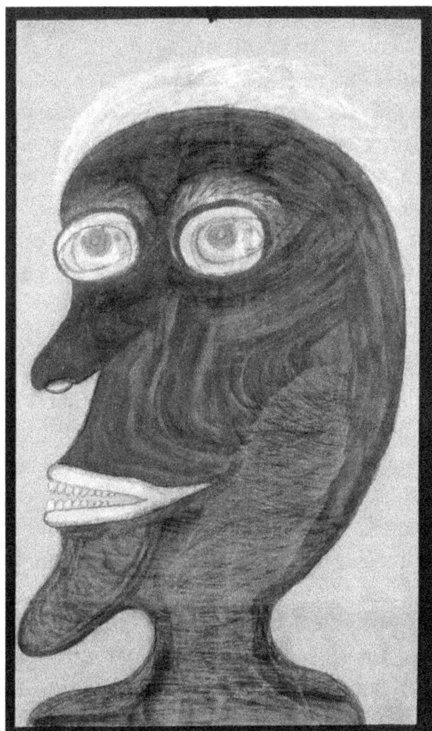

Figure 1.1 Heinrich Anton Müller, untitled, 1925–1927

Source: Courtesy Collection de l'Art Brut, Lausanne

disaffected with the art world and the art museum at its centre, arguing that it encouraged a narrow and repetitive elite of 'anointed' artists and ignored other, more creative artists from being recognised or seen.

They began to collect art produced outside the canon and experimented with alternative spaces that *would* show it. In America, as we shall see, anti-museum thinking was also deeply entrenched and gave rise to a proliferation of other forms. By the 1970s these initial impulses began to drive many artists, alongside similarly disaffected curator and collector allies, to find various ways of opposing conventional museology within, as well as beyond a museum building of some kind.

These are the main subject of this book.

Anti-museums were not the only museological change in the second half of the twentieth century. Change accelerated through the 1970s and

1980s when new forms of visitor experience and curatorial practice emerged within the conventional public museum sector in response to new demands to widen attendance, improve engagement, adopt new technologies and commercialise. In the emerging heritage museums, there was a shift away from the dominant culture's view of history to one shaped by popular culture, oral history, labour history and the everyday. Through negotiation with culturally diverse groups, the heritage museum became a less mediated experience and a more democratic space, converging with, rather than standing apart from, the communities they served (Witcomb 2003; Macdonald 2008). As a result, they thrived and their museum publics expanded. The same cannot be said for art museums.

For Radywyl et al. (2011), the 'new museology' produced little change beyond 'heightened participation' in most public art museums, and for the most part they remained steadfastly attached to a conventional curatorial offer, structured around academic art history and an improving stance/emphasis on 'educative leisure' (Prior 2002; Hanquinet & Savage 2012; Green 2018). In a period characterised by the rise and rise of contemporary art, this inevitably produced a tension with living artists, for whom the art history of their work was a lot less relevant than its subject matter and its intended social *impact*. Many prominent contemporary artists wanted to raise consciousness and effect social and political change through their work, yet frustratingly, the quietened, reverential gallery spaces and art historical emphasis side tracked visitors into anthology, taxonomy and chronology (Collings 2001; Judd 2016; Green 2018). Fine and important for researchers of art history, but were museums founded primarily for art history research or for the formation of broader art publics? The answer may be both, but arguably only the former thrived in the modern art museum.

Initially, a growing army of young, less prominent contemporary and outsider artists were ignored and left unseen by mainstream art museums. Living artists whether recognised or not, could not be ignored or wrapped up in history in the same way that dead artists had been, and they began to frame new types of alliances with a new generation of activist curators and collectors who often shared their frustrations. The ICA in London was founded by a group of intellectuals, artists and collectors (Cranfield 2008) and they were going to forge something other than an art museum in the conventional sense: 'an adult play centre, a workshop where work is a joy, a source of vitality and daring experiment' (Cranfield 2014). Anti-museums were typically founded by new mixes of enthusiast, including amateur collectors in league with artists.

What is an anti-museum?

How then, can a museum be both a museum and against museums? It seems impossible until it is appreciated how the modern museum has largely conformed to a very narrow set of aims, conventions and exhibitionary strategies, and that the aims of most anti-museums are often deliberately and diametrically opposed to them in some, or several, important respects (Berger 2018; Green 2018; Collings 2001). The anti-museum concept begins to make sense when one appreciates that modern museums came into being in the first place as an 'approved' and improving form of educative leisure, and as a form of cultural governance and politics at a time in the nineteenth century when northern Europe's lively and ubiquitous popular culture was being marginalised, discouraged, legislated against, emasculated or banished (Storch 1982; Reid 1982; Daunton 1983; Thompson 1992; Bennett 1995). Carnival had been popular in every village and town across Europe, but its enthusiastic patronage by the aristocracy waned after the French Revolution and their new-found fear of large crowds on city streets. Carnival was left exposed to the rising power of its long-time opponents, the protestant industrialists. In the remarkably short period between 1830 and 1900, carnival was banished almost everywhere, except southern Europe. Just how embedded and extensive art was in the popular cultural realm of carnival before then can be immediately grasped by the profoundly musical nature of London's streets in the mid-nineteenth century (Simpson 2015), by the depth of visual art, theatricality and comedy in carnival and by the constant reworking of traditional forms of expression addressed to contemporary political issues (Brewer 1979; Bristol 1983; Bruner 2005), all of it taking place in the public realm, and much of it constituting what Adorno (1999) meant by a public sphere. For Bakhtin (1984), here was the 'borderline between art and life', and it was produced by a community as a whole, mostly as free expression by individuals and local organisations.

In place of what protestant leaders considered the morally dubious, alcohol fuelled and wild antics of carnival – a period of festivities that reigned across a 'festive half-year', from Christmas to midsummer – a new raft of sober-minded, improving leisures were funded and built by Protestant captains of industry, and high on their list was the founding of museums, libraries and art galleries (Roud 2008; Collinson 2016; Franklin 2019). The link between the community and its expressive voice in art was thereby lost in the modern museum. Only the art by recognised and 'approved' academic artists was exhibited and only exceptionally would local artists be included; it was collected, curated and exhibited in order to narrate a linear and representative history tracing a developmental path of gradual improvement to the present day, in ways that validated the present and incumbent power; and its purpose was to impart an understanding of the individual artists as they were formed by, and contributed to this historical narrative of 'progress' (Bennett 1995). Chronology, taxonomy and didacticism were among its key organising principles and art history was the object of instruction and main purpose of the museum, apart from collection and conservation. The modern art gallery avoided the subjects of art and rendered less vibrant (or urgent) the expectation that art would explore how we might live better lives (Martin 2013; Adorno 1999; O'Connor 2010). As we have seen, almost all of its characteristics, and certainly its aims, have come in for significant criticism over a long period, especially from the artists, curators and collectors in the contemporary art period, so that the wonder is not that there are anti-museums, but why there are so few. The origins and history of these objections are described in the next section.

Origins

The anti-museum concept was conceived and in circulation from around the late eighteenth century. Initially, critics such as Quatremère de Quincy aimed to liberate the objects and artworks from the museum-as-mausoleum – from the way it disconnected them from their origins, contexts and their social life beyond the museum walls (Sherman 1994). At a later point, other critics wished to liberate those *subject* to its discipline, agency and authority (Maleuvre 1999), especially from the way museum collections were used as forms of memory to divine value, direct, and govern. This criticism focussed variously on the museum as a source of redemptive memory and refuge that stunted progress, or as a place of authoritative retrieval for the modern West's mythic/egoistic sense of its origins and superiority, or, as its privileged medium for reflection on the human condition (Maleuvre 1999; Butler 2016; Cleary 2006). As such, the anti-museum was proposed as an alternative to both the historic Alexandrina museum paradigm as well as the modern museum itself (Butler 2016; Sherman 1994).

The anti-museum thesis was advanced most radically as a critique of the exhibition of art in museums, as it gathered together concerns, from Quatremère de Quincy to Nietzsche, about the way art objects were thereby disconnected from contexts that give them meaning; from the complex relationships that art works always sustain with life outside the museum (which for some is their destiny), and from their potential for transformative, emotional energy and excitement (Sherman 1994; Huyssen 1986, p. 173). For the Futurists, an early twentieth century art movement with beginnings in Italy, museums were less a valued repository/resource of history than a distraction from the making of history. These were not minor quibbles. The anti-museum critique was vociferously opposed to museums as significant and momentous institutions of power and domination that negates rather than propagates art. They were to be burned and replaced by exhibitionary platforms (especially theatre and performance) where art might be reunited with life, a view recognising that the birth of the modern museum was directly connected with the killing of carnival and the West's rich popular culture (Bennett 1995; Bakhtin 1984; Marinetti 1909, pp. 189–190).

For some, the term anti-museum is an ill-defined genealogy of entities, variously considered ambiguous, contradictory or impossible to realise. Indeed, as Michaela Giebelhausen (2003) has shown, there are examples of the anti-museum thesis succeeding in the deliberate *refusal* to build national museums, a case in point being Brasilia which was subject to a thoroughgoing modernist design process. So, the anti-museum also has a life as an absence, and this is emphasised by a number of protest installations over the years from the USA to Germany and Japan (see Copeland & Balthazar 2017 for a compendium of examples), many taking the form of a permanently locked gallery.

More commonly, anti-museum sentiments were acted on by artists and took the form of new exhibitionary platforms, in new spaces and with new narratives (Lorente 2011; Smith 2012). Western contemporary artists had long been sources of criticism of public art museums, many setting up their own not-for-profit artspaces in conjunction with alternative/independent curators and private foundations such as Dia Foundation in the USA.

The modern museum's emphasis on art history was singularly problematic for the deadening, temporally dissociating exhibition of contemporary art, and many artists felt that their work was not best served by the contemplative, reverential, art historical and corporate cultures of the modern art gallery (as pioneered by MoMA [the Museum of Modern Art, New York) – especially in its ubiquitous white cube style of exhibition where any distractions from the art itself, emotional and otherwise, were removed or discouraged (Duncan & Wallach 1978; Lorente 2011; Maak et al. 2011). Characteristically, contemporary artists want to stimulate strong emotional responses from their publics and to focus attention on the subjects and social/political objects of their art, and thus they grew increasingly frustrated. Such sentiments prompted a move from reason/instruction to emotions/experience, especially in the not-for-profit art spaces and foundations they created (Foster 2015; Krauss 1990; Serota 2000; Smith 2012).

Activism

In the late 1960s, Donald Judd and others developed forms of 'anti-curation' and 'anti-museum'. For example, they moved single-artist sculptural exhibitions into spaces where the subjects of their art and its political and emotional impacts might be heightened (Goldberg 1980, p. 369; Lorente 2011). Judd himself moved away from the cultural centre and precinct to a high desert location at Marfa, Texas, the required journey purposely adding aspects of pilgrimage into the experience (see also Barush 2016). Others used theatrical devices, musical platforms or nightclub metaphors (e.g. PS1, New York). Judd never gave up his total opposition to the modern art museum, even during the period of 'New Museology'. In 1992, he gave us this: 'Almost all of the museums of Europe and America of the last decade are offensive' (Judd 2016, p. 785). His Chinati Foundation and Judd Foundation at Marfa are dedicated to a thoroughgoing reversal of conventional museum values, governance, aspirations and social/political orientations. It is a great favourite among artists and the travelling art public willing to set out for the middle of nowhere, but paradoxically few others have had the courage or resources to emulate it. As Thomas Kellein (2010, p. 8) wrote in the forward to *Chianti: The Vision of Donald Judd*, 'The values embodied in Judd's vision of his ideal art museum are enthusiastically embraced by many in the art world today, but they are far from prevalent …'.

Through the 1970s, anti-museums aimed to transform the role of art in society, refocus on the subjects and subjectivities of art, support artists themselves, revolutionise how art was exhibited and expand how art might be experienced and engaged with. There was a *lot* wrong with MoMA seemingly, and the critique ranged across aesthetic, historical, cultural, political, economic and social dimensions. Its apotheosis was felt most in the excitable, world-changing gestation of the Centre Pompidou, Paris, a cultural monument to the events of May 1968. The Pompidou Centre was to be a very 'new type of museum which would be entertaining, accessible, impermanent, free, anti-elitist, devoted equally to design as to fine art, to books and film and street theatre …' (Roberts 1997, p. 96; see also Duncan & Wallach 1978 and Saumarez Smith 1995). It kept up the ante, but only for a while. Eventually the same form of Presidential project that funded and cut through the conventional/conservative Parisian art establishment became the route by which it returned to the fold. It was not going to be the only time that global art world convention would contain, neutralise, co-opt or 'give canonic value to the those very things that set out to destroy the canon' (Roberts 1997, p. 97).

The anti-museums featured in this volume successfully attempted to break down the cultural politics and civilising mission of the modern museum, which, in the twentieth century development of MoMA, had become a conservative, politically controlled voice of corporate America. The capacity of artists and art to excite, incite, challenge and transform were tranquilised in its silent and bleached white interiors. This was art as political asylum/exile. It was challenged increasingly and experimentally. Some realised that to succeed they needed to detach themselves from governments and government sources of funding. Museums are very expensive. This is why there are so few anti-museums and why those that succeeded have something extraordinary about them: they have very resourceful, charismatic and courageous individuals at their centre.

Contemporary

The yBas group (young British artists) took to curating and exhibiting their own shows in the wake of the near total collapse of the London gallery sector in 1990, mostly outside conventional art museum aims and formats (Stallybrass 2006). Prior to the dramatic expansion and growth of contemporary art after 2000, alternative non-didactic exhibitionary and collecting cultures for contemporary art became a built-in element for much art practice. It was the eventual florescence of contemporary art after 2000 and its shift from being a marginal, esoteric and self-referential genre to being mainstream popular culture, that offered the possibility for these exhibitionary models to become normative and realised in a number of new forms and, especially scales. Out of this, some would raise the anti-museum flag once more.

Anti-museum formats and the thinking behind them also emerged from a time of crisis in the art world. In the mid-2000s art critics issued gloomy prognoses on the future of what they call 'institutional critique', when all art appeared to be implicated and fatally compromised through its co-option by art world institutions, its rampant commercialisation, its massive expansion on the back of windfalls from the global financial crisis and its growing dependency on a wealthy collecting elite. At first, the dramatic rise of contemporary art alongside austerity measures imposed on public art museums created a panic. As Fraser (2005) argued, 'there no longer is an outside' from which to mount a critique.

> How, then, can we imagine, much less accomplish, a critique of art institutions when museum and market have grown into an all-encompassing apparatus of cultural reification? Now, when we need it most, institutional critique is dead, a victim of its success or failure, swallowed up by the institution it stood against.
>
> (p. 279)

Far from being emasculated through institutionalisation, Fraser sensed a source of strength:

> It's not a question of being against the institution: We are the institution. It's a question of what kind of institution we are, what kind of values we institutionalize, what forms of practice we reward, and what kinds of rewards we aspire to. Because the institution of art is internalized, embodied, and performed by individuals, these are the questions that institutional critique demands we ask, above all, of ourselves.
>
> (p. 280)

Better late than never.

Art museum developments since then increasingly took the form of artists, curators, collectors and institutions taking up this pragmatic stance for reinvention (Smith 2012; Hanquinet & Savage 2012; Franklin & Papastergiadis 2017), and over the past ten years we have seen an expanded version of the 'exhibitionary complex' emerge, often developing alternative, fringe or festive models (Bennett 1988; Smith 2012).

Ironically, significant contemporary artists and their galleries began to adopt *these* models as public art museums became unable to provide the necessary public exposure necessary to maintain their reputations. The dramatic rise in contemporary art prices, combined with budgetary cuts in the public art museum sector, meant that the latter could no longer sustain previous collecting levels (Franklin 2020). Instead, contemporary artists turned to exchanging their best works for exposure in a new generation of private/independent museums and art spaces that were more artist-focussed (see Heckmüller 2011). These artists gained exhibitionary and curatorial collaborations they had never had before, and collectors gained creative and expressive roles beyond the silent partner provisions of the Getty era (Franklin and Papastergiadis 2017; Terry Smith (2009, 2012).

Contemporary art also began to be a more distributed into everyday spaces of hotels, bars, shop windows and public spaces. Laurie Hanquinet and Mike Savage (2012, p. 52) found that new exhibitionary platforms generated new dispositions and new art publics with antipathy to conventional art museums: 'the more a museum presents itself as a traditional educational place, the more it will be criticised for its detachment from the spectators, the rest of society and from ordinary life'. More youthful and creative audiences preferred art museums with 'a "figural" sensitivity based on a visual immersion rather than a "discursive" sensitivity based on a priority of words over images, a rationalist view of culture and a distancing of the spectator from the cultural object' (ibid., p. 52).

Contemporary art since 2000 increasingly abandoned 'art about art' that had been popular with conventional art museums, in favour of art relevant to pressing issues of their times. Hal Foster (2015) identified five themes of the new contemporary art: the abject, the precarious, the traumatic, the archival and the lost. These symptomatic objects of what he called (after Brecht) the 'bad new days' of neoliberal ascendency are often addressed through the carnivalesque techniques of 'mimetic exacerbation' and 'mockery' that reach directly to knowing popular audiences through their own bodies. Against the grain, Foster tells us that 'the avant-garde is alive and well'. Not attempting the transgression of a given order or the legislation of a new one, the avant-garde that interests him now is 'immanent in a caustic way': 'it seeks to trace fractures that already exist within the given order, to pressure them further, to activate them somehow' (p. 284).

Beyond the cultural precinct

The spatial periphery, former industrial zones and other spaces on the social margin became a new ecological niche for anti-museums. Requiring out-of-the-way touristic journeys, separation from the everyday and demanding significant commitments of time, these locations are often chosen to foster receptivity to new ideas and enhance more sensual encounters with art (Franklin 2014; Smith 2009).

David Walsh's Mona combined both extremes: a remote, former convict island and a rustbelt industrial area in the island state of Tasmania, Australia. The success he has had attracting people from across Australia, and internationally, to make a journey specifically to Mona raises the prospect of pilgrimage-like journeys, where, like the Grand Tour before it, the experience of art is conjoined with personal quests for redemption, release, play and adventure (McCarthy 2018). In 2011, *The Sunday Times* announced that, 'Mona is the most exciting addition to the Australian cultural landscape since the Sydney Opera House' (Parris 2011). On the back of this and other accolades, Lonely Planet ranked Hobart the seventh best city in the world to visit in 2013 and Mona the best art gallery in 2015.

The Museum of Everything is a travelling concept, taking the works by 'unintentional, untrained and undiscovered' artists into new kinds of spaces such as Selfridges' famous shop windows on Oxford Street, or the Chalet Society, Paris, a Catholic seminary-turned-exhibition space located in Saint-Germain (Snell 2017). Banksy also now travels collections of his works into anti-museum installations such as Dismaland, in the down-on-its luck seaside town of Western-super-Mare, UK; or the more permanent (real) colonial themed *Walled Off Hotel*, Bethlehem, a hotel that boasts the worst hotel view in the world – a lookout over the barrier wall separating

Israeli and the Palestinian territories, with glimpses of Israeli army watch towers.

Anti-museums readily breach their own museum walls. La Collection de l'Art Brut stages outdoor exhibition in its own park; PS1 has brought music and a club atmosphere into its former playground spaces; Art42 has taken its art across France and now has an exhibition mooring on the Seine. Mona is perhaps the exemplar museum for taking its anti-museology beyond the museum walls. Its estate grounds at Moorilla are an active and important space where music, food and art are combined in new ways, around a major soundstage; around a weekend market format; at every opening (when, Great Gatsby-like, the entire city is invited rather than just the good and the great); at dusk/night around their major James Turrell *Amarna* 2015 installation; and as one of their festival venues. Across the Cities of Hobart and Glenorchy and into the hinterlands, their festivals, Mona Foma and Dark Mofo, extend their penetration and engagement into churches and chapels, beaches, underground cellars, industrial dockside buildings, an abandoned psychiatric hospital, theatres, churches, a reused 1950s cinema, back streets, public market areas and sacred war memorial grounds. In 2018, 418,963 travelled to see Dark Mofo, which compares with Glastonbury's 2016 attendance of 177,000 and the Edinburgh Festival's 2016 attendance of 450,000 (McKay and Webster 2016). The extent of collaboration and engagement across the city has been infectious. Government and business buildings are lit red during Dark Mofo and an impromptu/pop-up fringe builds steadily, alongside the progressive abandonment of city and street regulations that prevented/controlled free expression in the city since the nineteenth century. This rendering of the art museum into everyday space is significant, inclusive and critical. As Cranfield (2014) observed in relation to other such initiatives:

> For an institution that has frequently been associated with temperance and reserve, the less-than-sober excess of the museum, spilling out of its frame onto the streets and across time and space, threatens the stability of the institutional form that aims at hermetic separation from the contingency of the everyday.

Mona was announced as an anti-museum, designed as an anti-museum, and has offered a road-testing of the idea of an anti-museum as a viable mainstream museum format that was not so easily corrupted as the Centre Pompidou. Being a private venture, owned by one man, meant that conventional political and governmental pressures were eliminated, while not preventing co-funding and other partnerships with governments and governmental organisations at every level.

Darkness

Anti-museums have a tendency to avoid light, as much as they avoid seeking only to enlighten. Nightclubs were a bigger influence on PS1's founder Alanna Heiss than other museums and for many years PS1 was the only non-profit member of the New York Nightlife Association (Miller 2016). Mona and some of its imitators (e.g. the Tasmanian Museum and Art Gallery; Prada Milan) have gone underground or turned off the emotionally neutral light of the white cube. Theirs is a more mysterious gloaming or twilight catacomb. They also turn up the sound and include more music and smell. They seek to transform and enliven rather than instruct. They want people to be lost rather than saved. They appeal to non-art audiences who connect to them via music, popular culture, fashion and politics, as well as art scene types bored of traipsing around museum spaces designed to exact quietude and reverence. Perhaps the most radical of the anti-museums was a form of exhibition created for 'l'art brut', first in 1940s Paris and later in Lausanne, Switzerland, in the 1970s. Art brut was first championed by Jean Dubuffet who defined it as

> anything produced by people unbesmirched by artistic culture, in which mimicry, contrary to what occurs with intellectuals, has little or no part. So that the makers (in regard to subjects, choice of materials employed, means of transposition, rhythms, ways of writing, etc.) draw entirely on their own resources rather than on the sterotypes of classical or fashionable art.
>
> (Dubuffet 1949, p. 8)

Here, darkness was a key trope – in two senses. Originally Dubuffet was attracted to the art of inmates of mental hospitals, prisons and orphanages, and his first exhibitions, under the guise of *Le Foyer de l'Art Brut* (1947), in the basement of the Galerie Drouin in Paris, were held in secret. The works were hung in a detached manner, to heighten their sense of displacement, repulsion and exile (Thévoz 1975), though it was only when his collection found its final home at the Château de Beaulieu in Lausanne that he began using the term anti-museum (Rousseau 2010, p. 71). At Lausanne, the curator Michel Thévoz used black or darkened walls, which surprised and then delighted Dubuffet. It resonated with 'anti-culture', his other much favoured term, and a view that 'cultural art in its entirety appears to be the game of a futile society, a fallacious parade' (Merrick 2010).

As Dubuffet's collection expanded to elaborate the scope of 'outsider artists', he denounced the modern museum as 'morgues for embalming' or pompous 'citadels of official culture'. Art brut was less easy to assimilate back into the modern museum and the idea continues to drive significant

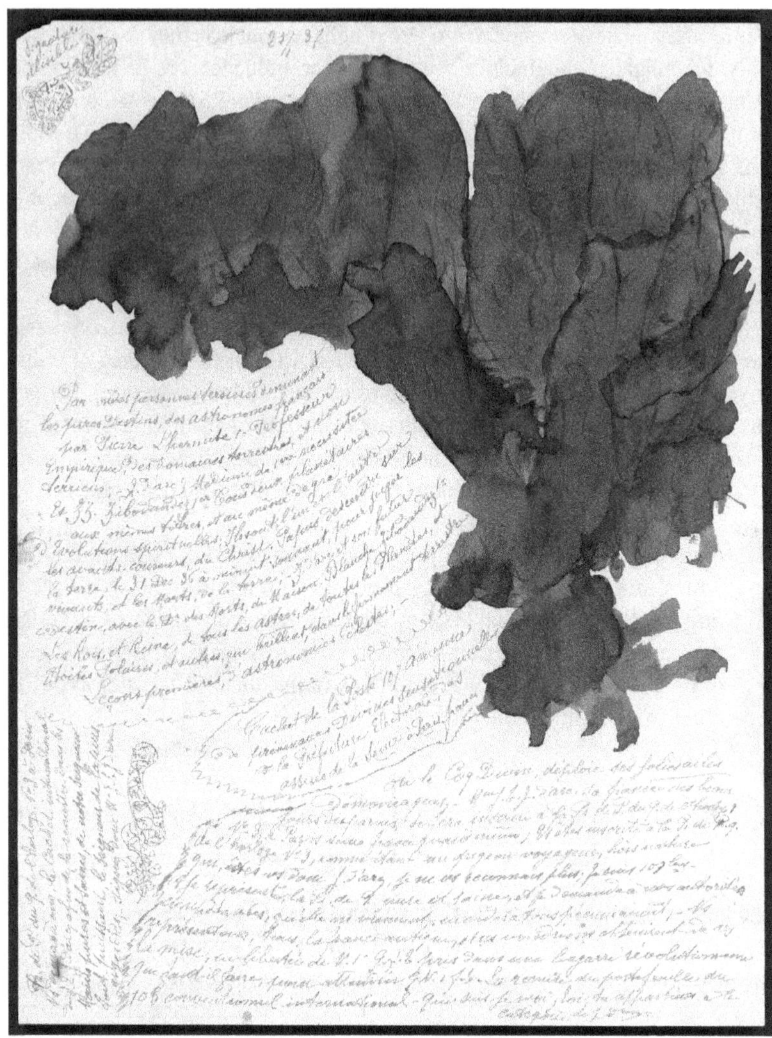

Figure 1.2 Jeanne Tripier, untitled, 25 January 1937

Source: Courtesy Collection de l'Art Brut, Lausanne

museological innovation such as James Brett's Museum of Everything (MoE).

Inspired by Art Brut, MoE extended such outsider art even further, not least for being a travelling exhibitionary format that pops up in random special places around the world with great success. Here again, another individual collector, James Brett, likes to exhibit dark or dimly lit corners or rooms, the trope of modest home spaces being more favoured than gallery cubes. But Brett likes to surprise too and to place works by these artists in high status windows (literally) for irony and juxtaposition. In 2011, for example, MoE occupied spaces in one the world's most commercial temples of consumerism. At Selfridges, in Oxford St, *Exhibition #4* invaded its famous shop windows, its *Wonder Room* and its dimmer basement areas – attracting 100,000 people in a ten-week run (Museum of Everything 2011). Next to the most glamorous commercial brands in the world, displayed by the very best art-window dressers, it showed 'the first global survey of studios for self-taught artists with developmental disabilities' (Museum of Everything 2011, p. 11). Then, in 2017 it moved its considerable collection of outsider art/art brut to be the annual centrepiece exhibition at Mona, some 56 feet below ground (17 metres) in the murky depths of its catacombs. At Mona, design maven Adrian Spinks created something like Brett's childhood home inside their international touring exhibition space.

Humour and play

Anti-museums also tend to oppose conventional modern museums by avoiding the seriousness with which they present art and the serious atmosphere in which visitors are expected to engage with it. If theatre, opera, other live music and cinema audiences can be animated and emotional in their response to, and engagement with art, why must the viewing of painting or sculpture be done in such controlled emotional settings, with audiences hushed and physically undemonstrative (and saddled with learning aids)? Many anti-museums actively oppose the seriousness of conventional museums by injecting humour into the museum experience – frequently by including humorous works with serious objectives – but also in their museum's communications, aimed, directly or indirectly, at the art world, or even its own art. Bakhtin (1984) made the point that authority of all kinds is not only serious, it lacks a sense of humour. Mona takes this a stage further in the clowning antics of its museum owner, David Walsh and writer Elizabeth Pearce (Franklin 2014) and 'clowning' is to be found as much in their communications, digital platforms and social media sites as it is in their museum language, design and anti-catalogues (catalogues that are critical and satirical rather than boosterish).

For Bakhtin, seriousness was something that always rendered authority, and those who aspire to it, vulnerable to mockery and satire, creating a powerful space of critique and the possibility of a critical public sphere that was always part of popular culture. A mocking stance to the seriousness of art was Mona's means of liberating it, but perhaps more importantly a means of reaching out to a wider public who, they felt were needlessly intimidated and alienated from it. Whereas art gallery catalogues are almost invariably talking up the importance of their works, in earnest, serious tones, we get the opposite in Mona catalogues. If it is not always mocking or satirical, it never misses opportunities to raise *doubt* with alternative voices as a counterpoint to art's self-assuredness. To ram home the point that they are not art establishment, the conventional art voice/art history is parodied at Mona by tactlessly labelling it 'artwank'. Art history is not dismissed, it has a say, but it is not given the final word. That is left up to a viewing public to work through from choices and an absence of direction. This level of trust in a viewing public is also a feature of the anti-museums featured in this book. We find humour prominent in our consideration of other anti-museums: at The New Museum, New York; in the street art of Art42, Paris; and in the content and presentation of outsider art at The Museum of Everything (London).

Monty Python's Flying Circus, a uniquely surreal ('Pythonesque') sketch show, made a point of targeting the idiosyncrasies/anachronisms of British professional culture and they lost no time in framing the art gallery – the 'Art Gallery sketch' appeared in their fourth episode, *Owl-Stretching Time*, first aired in the UK on 26 October 1969. Monty Python found the art gallery a perfect object of ridicule for satire and mockery. It featured two 'uneducated' working class housewives [played by men in drag], with young children in tow, discussing art with well-formed taste, appreciation and connoisseurship, interrupted only by one of their children who had developed a taste for fine art, by actually eating it. Those who never go to art galleries and do not understand art laugh the loudest when they see themselves represented as espousing the pompous language of expertise and taste while attempting to prevent their child from eating priceless artworks. I did. I was 13 in October in 1969, and knew nothing about art or the art world but I got the joke, or enough of it to realise it was poking fun at art museums; that 'art' was not part of my everyday world, but an esoteric world belonging to transcendent, remote experts. This humour is therefore inclusive, since, whether one was a gallery-goer or not, it is clear that the sketch pokes fun at an obscure and snobbish art world and the somewhat pitiful bids for social distinction it encourages. Monty Python's are not the only artists to deploy laughter against art. Citing Callum Storrie's *Delirious Museum* (2006), Ben Cranfield (2014) recounts how artists, from Dadaism to Surrealism used humour to critique the modern art museum:

> The humorous and the playful were used to oppose the rigidity of culture exemplified by the hallowed spaces of the Louvre, most notably in Duchamp's defacement of a postcard of the Mona Lisa with the addition of a moustache and the letters L.H.O.O.Q. which, when read out loud in French, supposedly translates as 'she has a hot ass'.

Duchamp famously also staged the theft of the *Mona Lisa* from the Louvre.

Playfulness and play was deliberately inserted into the early and later content of the Institute for Contemporary Arts, London, in order to reconnect art to its original base in ritual, as an active, transformative, collective and pleasurable part of life. The modern museum tends to atomise emotionally neutralised individuals as well as hive playfulness off into separate museum areas for children, but anti-museums have reversed this in many cases (Cranfield 2013; Franklin & Sansom 2018).

Six case studies

In the remaining chapters a critical exploration of five anti-museum case studies is undertaken. The case studies span their early and mid-twentieth century beginnings in new art movements and counter-cultural politics and their continuing presence in new international settings for contemporary art. Each case study chapter will chart their background, aims, development and evolution in more detail. Each chapter documents what they do in the contemporary world, what they are against, and how they have innovated new solutions to old problems by reversing the orderings of the conventional modern museum. In each case, it is shown how they engage their publics in new ways, within and beyond the museum walls; and how they respond to the particularities of the changing world around them.

Each chapter will evaluate the difference they have made to our engagement with art and assess the extent to which their presence, their success and their collaborations have impacted on the conventional art museum establishment – whether they have shifted taste, ethics, aesthetics, engagement, atmosphere and what counts as art.

It will also analyse how their operations fit into the cultural ecology of their locations and settings, and whether they can remain commercially viable, as well as philanthropically connected, to their traditional public partners. It will analyse their contribution to the life of their communities, the vibrancy of local arts and their value to the travelling art public – to traveling artists as well as art tourists. By showing the extent of their diversity and changes of approach, the book offers those looking beyond convention a wide range of inspiration and choice.

With a renewed emphasis on experimentation and fluidity, the tide has changed for the anti-museum. In the shape of The Chinati Foundation and Judd Foundation at Marfa, Texas; at PS1 and the New Museum in New York, at the Collection de l'Art Brut, Lausanne, Switzerland; at Art42 in Paris and at Mona in Tasmania, Australia, the anti-museum proves to be as resilient as it is variable.

By definition, the conventional modern museum has a remarkably predictable *form* and offers a largely standard experience. Many museums of art offer essentially similar collections too. The same cannot be said for anti-museums. They tend not to be located in the central places favoured by conventional museums; they tend not to follow the grandly authoritative statements of conventional architecture, they tend not to follow the same exhibitionary design strategies, language or display and they tend to have very specific types of collection. Each anti-museum reverses these conventions in unique ways. For these reasons, a first-person account of arriving into, and encountering each of the anti-museum case studies will be given. Readers will gain a sense of the areas they are in; how visitors are received; the architecture that houses them; the ambience inside the museum; the different ways of seeing art in them and how other visitors appear to engage with them.

2 Collection de l'Art Brut, Lausanne

Introduction

After the steep ascent of L'Avenue de Beaulieu from the old town centre of Lausanne, the left turn at the top follows a high ridge with spectacular views over the city. It's an elegant avenue, leading out to further hills, suitably named Avenue des Bergières. Here, are especially large houses in their own grounds, the most notable being Chateau Beaulieu (built between

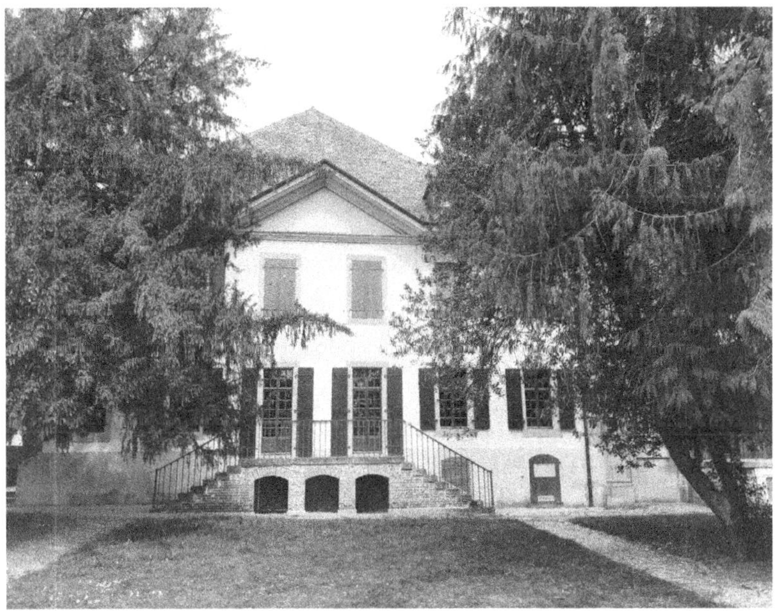

Figure 2.1 Chateau Beaulieu, Lausanne

Photo: Adrian Franklin

1764 and 1776). Opening up behind it is the space of a small linear walk through what was once the lower terrace of its garden, now called the *Parc et Promenade de Chateau Beaulieu*. This is a noted scenic look-out and in the nearby streets below there are good places for lunch and dinner.

Chateau Beaulieu had fallen into the hands of the City of Lausanne, and they bequeathed it to house a significant collection of 'art brut' (raw art), donated to the city in 1971 by the prominent French artist, Jean Dubuffet. He had selected the city as a site worthy of his plan to exhibit it publicly and permanently for the very first time. *L'art brut*, was created by non-professional, untaught or self-taught artists, often those living in asylums, hospitals, prisons, or on the streets, without any aim to exhibit or garner a reputation as an artist (Rousseau 2018). As far as conventional art museums were concerned it was illegitimate art, and never shown, but Dubuffet thought it had the power to change the way we think about art forever.

For Dubuffet, his discovery of art brut (first during the 1940s at several psychiatric hospitals in Switzerland) had momentous implications for the art world when the notion of the artist as an 'extraordinary genius' was coming under increasing scrutiny and doubt (Fol 2015, p. 63). Dubuffet's early career idealism included a critique of the professional artist as one who mostly copies, follows and conforms rather than 'creates'. As Fol (2015) puts it, he wished to avoid the 'integration, filiation and propagation' that was symptomatic of the art world and had been so for a long time (see, for example, Marshall 2016). By comparison, art brut artists were radically independent of intellectual patronage and influence. They created work that responded directly, and only to the conditions of their lives and with no thought for how it would be received by others, or even *whether* it would ever be viewed by anyone other than themselves. They never anticipated or addressed (or were constrained by) the judgement of others, or by a viewing, paying public or an investing market. The materials they used, their subject matter, the objects of their art and their tools and techniques, all emanated from the contexts and events of their life and experience. Consequently, their works were often more open, freer and uncensored in ways that professional artists' works were not. They were especially freer in their expression of feelings, drives and emotions as they impacted the body, and thus collectively, they pioneered a fearless exploration of mind, body, self and society.

Conversely, 'academic artists' were held in the gravity of cultural convention by those with the power to judge them against an arbitrary canon of public exhibition and art history: the curators, critics and governing bodies of elite art museums. Through their tight control of exhibition and acceptance into their academies and collections, they were also able to determine which art was worthy of public display, admiration and acclaim. As a result, artists inevitably made art for their approval and judgement rather than as it should be, in Dubuffet's view, a spontaneous and true reaction to, and critique, of their life and times. In Dubuffet's view, this was something that all museums should encourage, but had collectively failed to do. In Dubuffet's hands, art brut was rendered into a critique of academic art which would always undermine it and eventually, he predicted, change it. He also believed it would change museology and museum experience.

Dubuffet's collection at Chateau Beaulieu was deliberately never called a museum, instead it has always been called La Collection de l'Art Brut (hereafter CDLAB). Opened in 1976, it was the first museum dedicated to art brut in the world and is still the single largest collection and the most influential (Sarah Lombardi cited in Laird 2018). Throughout its significant history it has been consistently referred to as an anti-museum, or in French, *un anti-musée* (Thévoz 1994; Peiry 2001, pp. 177–225; Mintern 2007; Maclagan 2010; Rousseau 2018).

According to Peiry (2001), while Dubuffet and CDLAB's first curator Michel Thévoz understood that ideally, this art should not be publicly

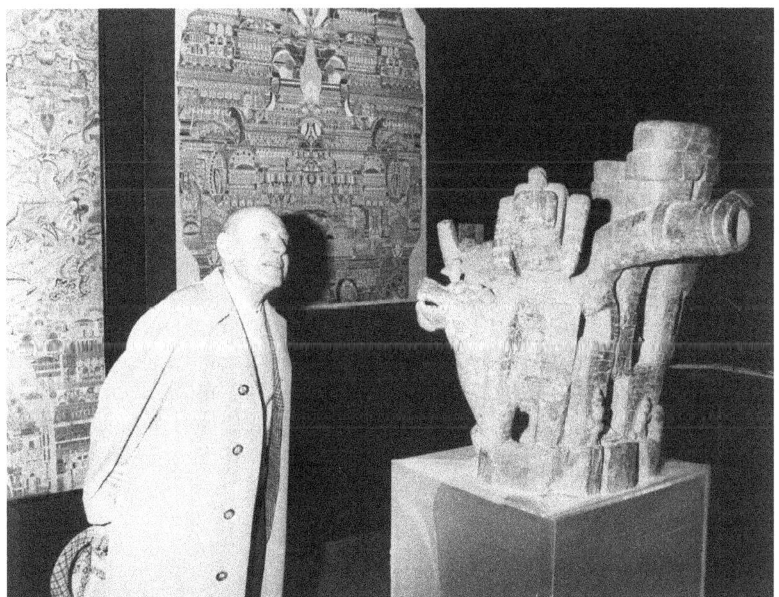

Figure 2.2 Jean Dubuffet in the Collection de l'Art Brut, February 1976

Photo: Jean-Jacques Laeser

exhibited, they also felt (paradoxically) that it was essential they do so to unleash its power to highlight a major problem with cultural art institutions. It was therefore a gamble on art brut's 'contentious power to react on the medium at which, and on which they were being exhibited' (Peiry 2001, p. 178):

> Art brut, amounted to putting the museum in crisis, showing the visitor, which is to say the common man [*sic*], the anthropological potentialities of expression which enculturation had led him to abandon.... The art brut collection thus really does highlight a pathology of art.
>
> (Michel Thévoz *Requiem pour la folie*, 1995, p. 67)

While art brut was admirable and inspiring to Dubuffet and his followers, they understood the dangers of allowing it to come under the gravitational pull of the art world and so maintained its separation categorically and physically. It was so completely removed from, and unaffected by the art world, its academy, its markets and publics, that Dubuffet felt strongly that their work should never be framed or interpreted by its institutional structures. This is one reason why his collection came to Lausanne rather than stay in Paris, the more obvious choice perhaps, and where it might have a had a more significant and immediate impact. Another reason was that the art brut Dubuffet first found was in the French-speaking cantons of Switzerland. To repatriate his collection there made good sense: the collection was born from the culture and history of its peoples who were naturally more rebellious and anti-authority than the conventional Parisian art world. He wanted a space specially orientated to it where 'neither psychiatric nor cultural institutions could intervene' (Fol 2015, p. 108). While the French Ministry of Culture was the natural entity to receive such a collection, they had only offered to dedicate 'some' space to it in the new museum being built in Beaubourg, Paris (The Pompidou Centre). Another offer, from the Musée des Arts Decoratifs in Paris, was also unacceptable to Dubuffet for similar reasons. They would not undertake to put it all on display, which would have fragmented it as a collection. Dubuffet also felt uneasy about his collection being swallowed up by what he called 'an official museum' (Fol 2015, p. 107).

Exhibition in the dark

The other option then, was to develop an alternative kind of institution/exhibitionary platform that was dedicated to art brut; to establish in it a permanent reference collection; to actively search out new works from different circumstances and places, and to inaugurate alternative research narratives. Establishing the Collection de l'Art Brut was therefore an exhibitionary contradiction of sorts. These works were made explicitly and solely for their makers in whose lives they were functionally supportive and transformative (Fol 2015, p. 108). How might a viewing public, estranged from the circumstances of their origins, relate to them in a meaningful way? How were works that were not meant to be shown to the public to be presented publicly by their champions? The answer: in the shadows and twilight of a darkened gallery.

The darkened walls and half-light created for the CDLAB has always caused some comment and speculation. Michel Thevot, argued that their dimly lit galleries with art hung against walls painted black was entirely driven by the frailty of the materials and mediums, to protect them from damaging strong light, but the art critic Preszow felt that their style of scenography was deployed to *dramatise*. Why were the works embellished by such lighting? Did not a darkened environment suggest dark subject matter, with the risk that it be confused with the sensationalism of fairground and peepshow?

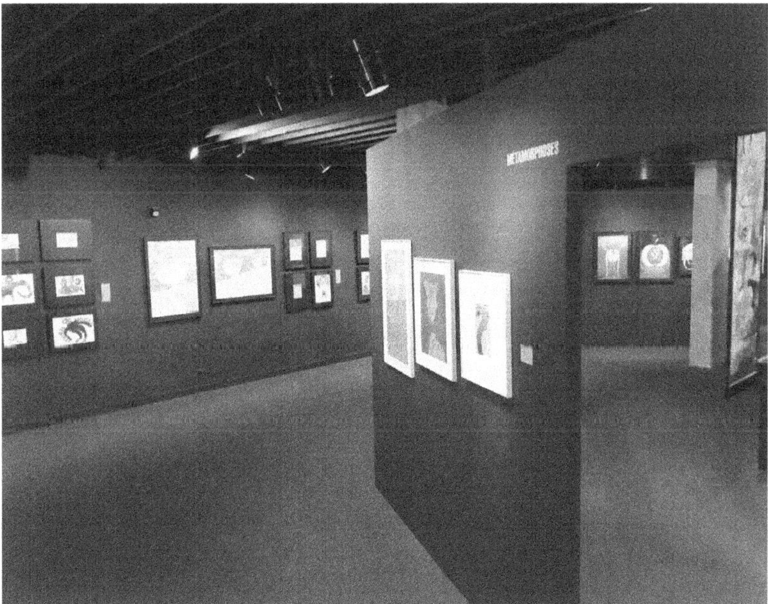

Figure 2.3 Darkened gallery

Photo: Adrian Franklin

Perhaps though, it was the other way around: that the exhibition of art should not avoid or stifle emotion through the neutral lighting of the ubiquitous white cube, but do the exact reverse. That emotion is precisely the vehicle through which *this* art should be experienced; that connections to it might be triggered by encountering it directly through its emotional charge. Fol (2015), for example, thought that their conserving scenography was at least *also* a device to engender immersion, engagement, and empathy with the artist whose life and social world were seen as keys to appreciating their artistic expression. Sarah Lombardi, the current Director, told me that she was frequently asked about the dark background and why she had not changed it to white or a lighter colour. After considering a possible change, she decided to stay with the black for yet other reason:

> I think it's good to remain with darkness because when a visitor enters the museum, and they go into this space, which is different, they understand that they're in a very special place which is not an everyday museum, not a fine art museum.... So, it marks a difference, as soon as you get inside, and you see that the space is different, the light is different and so it gives you the idea that you have to see these works with another gaze.
>
> (Interview with Sarah Lombardi, 11 December 2018)

Originally, the dimly lit works at the Lausanne collection were accompanied by brief medical, personal and sociological biographies and Thévoz claimed that visitors to CDLAB did connect to the artists, that they were touched and moved by what they saw; they were able to relate in some ways to its expression and content (Thévoz 1995). While perfectly plausible, I needed more than claims to be sure. To date no visitor survey has been conducted at CDLAB, so in lieu of that I decided to spend two days observing the museum and its visitors.

Visiting the Collection de l'Art Brut

When I first visited CDLAB, in April 2017, I was interested to see what kind of impression the art and its exhibitionary style would make on me, and on other visitors. Would our gaze be radically different? Would the experience be different from mainstream art museums? How would people comport themselves in its distinctive atmosphere and darkened interiors? Would seeing art brut at CDLAB be different from seeing the same types of art brut exhibited more conventionally – for example at the Lille Métropole Museum of Modern, Contemporary and Outsider Art (LaM), which I had visited previously? Was the anti-museological stance of Dubuffet still *channelled* at Lausanne?

I had a full two days to spend in Chateau de Beaulieu and three floors of art brut to encounter. Arriving some ten minutes before CDLAB opened I was able to study how they communicated such a complex notion as art brut to a passing, or an arriving, general public. Lausanne has a very significant visitor population (e.g. some 236,636 non-Swiss individuals stayed in Lausanne hotels in 2017) and as one of its more prominent, if not infamous, cultural institutions they could expect a significant proportion to turn up at their door (Schweizer Tourismus-Verband 2017).

As if still anticipating *some* trepidation, discomfort or incomprehension, their museum forecourt communications are kept simple, and minimal. One freestanding sign at the front of the museum boldly affirms a Dubuffet hero statement:

> L'art brut c'est l'art brut
> et tout le monde a très bien compris.
> Pas tout à fait très bien?
> Bien sûr, c'est pour ça justement
> qu'on est curieux d'y aller voir.
>
> [Raw art is raw art
> and the whole world has understood it well.
> If not perfectly?
> Of course, and to do it justice
> Is why we are so curious to see it.]
>
> (Dubuffet 1949)

Curiosity is a powerful motive for exploration. Dubuffet's riddle suggests that, unlike academic/conventional art, all people can understand or at least relate to art brut. They do not need special education and it does not need to be 'explained'. It is accessible to everyone at some level and we can all identify with the artists and their art on a deep emotional level, even if much of it is strange and personal and from unknown times and places. Dubuffet referred to the makers of art brut as 'authors' rather than artists and did not want their work to be assimilated into the 'art' canon. Much of their work is narrative and explicit rather than abstract, or deeply encoded. The Dubuffet quote says that we share in the humanity of art brut and yet of course we cannot already know the detail, and the connections back the lives of its authors; which is why we are so curious, compelled to see it, to find some answers. There's plenty for visitors to do there.

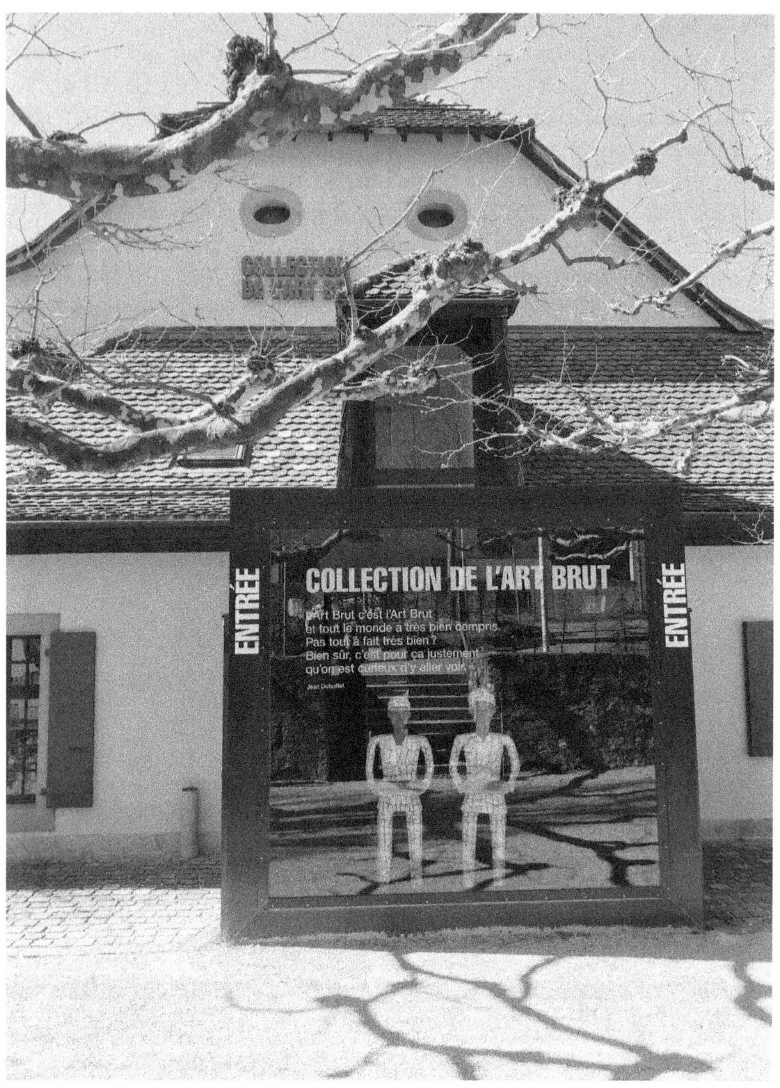

Figure 2.4 Entrance

Photo: Adrian Franklin

Figure 2.5 Exhibition poster
Photo: Adrian Franklin

A museum tour

I entered the Collection, not through the Chateau's original grand doors (those would not be in the anti-museum style), but through a small aperture that the architects called an 'airlock'. It's a very modest architectural addition: a metal framed structure, painted bronze, that holds darkly smoked plate glass windows with just a very small door to one side. Inside the airlock, the colour and texture changed to the dark slate grey of its walls, thickly padded with what looked like wire wool, but was obviously some kind of a man-made fibre. It may simply have been exposed insulation of course, but in scale and texture it looked most like a 'padded cell', something that might have been a suitable architectural metaphor for an art museum where so many of its works were produced in solitary confinement in psychiatric asylums/prisons/orphanages and other places of institutionalised exile.

Through the airlock door into the museum space, the light remains dim and the walls shift slightly to a very dark charcoal. Off to the right we can make out the bright colours of some of the art works in little pools of light, picked out by a busy legion of ceiling mounted spotlights. The spotlighting is theatrical, and sets up anticipation and attention. The net effect of the lighting is to create darkened spaces of intimacy around each work, so that it feels as if one is alone with the work in a tiny room. Indeed, this is picked up and respected by others. It is noticeable how, when one person (or a pair) occupy the space around a single work, other visitors tend not to stand alongside them, as is often the case in a neutrally lit white cube set-up. Intimacy is further stimulated by grouped works of a single or related artists being hung in small, semi-discrete spaces. Indeed, the entire museum is divided into little corners, nooks, bays and alcoves, something that works well with the generally small scale of the individual works.

Intimacy breeds attention at CDLAB and I was struck by how long visitors remained with many of the works. Attention is also generated and sustained by being alone with the work in the absence of any individual labels – which always risks closing off lines of spontaneously generated thought. Attention is the first kind of engagement I noticed, and it was a fairly close attention, driven by curiosity and wonderment. Art brut works almost invariably appear strange and otherworldly and they take time to establish any kind of descriptive or narrative sense. They are also often highly detailed, and that also takes time to assimilate. It was only if the viewer was inclined to know more that this was then followed by *inquiry* – reading the detailed biographical notes on the artists and how they came to make art. These were supplied on white-on-black notice boards close to, but not in the same frame of vision as the works. Most were in the area preceding their hang and it was common to see people return to them for a first or a second read.

Peiry (2001) (a former Director) is at pains to point out their wish to *underdetermine* the experience visitors have at CDLAB:

> Today the museum does not offer guided tours with prearranged itineraries, 'For what we have is a drunken boat that doesn't lend itself to being steered' (Thévoz 1991; 1993). No debates are organised, no conferences are scheduled: in keeping with the neutrality sought for the presentation of the works, this decision is in agreement with the desire to avoid conditioning people, manipulating them, preparing a message and presenting it.
>
> (Peiry 2001, p. 192)

The first section of the exhibition, *3ème Biennale de l'Art Brut: Corps*, was sub-titled *Métamorphoses*. Many of the works were transformational human bodies in liminal states, or human-non-human hybrids, and most of them seemed surreal initially. The first three works were very convincing, polished stylised paintings by the French woman Marguerite Burnat-Provins, all of them human–nature hybrids – human–bird, human–insect and human–feline with human faces. Stranger still, the next group by Sylvain Lecocq, a 50-year-old French man, were crude drawings on scrap paper of urinating humanoids; one a futuristic cyborg, the other a human with a smiling radish head. Equally strange were surreal figures by the American Charles Steffen, including a reclining female vegetal–human nude, and another of a sunflower and a slightly puckish child, entitled *Mother and Child, Sunflower Nude*. Both drawings are annotated with text, dedicating the works to the memory of a lost friend and a deceased mother, and both are vaguely sexualised. As I later discovered the puckish youth had a strong likeness to a photo of Charles. Next, there was a panel of brightly painted works by the octogenarian Ghanaian artist Ataa Oko. All of the paintings feature human–animal hybrids: a human–butterfly, several human–fish and a human–bird. Many of them are female with crudely painted breasts. One is a female figure lying on the ground being washed or, possibly, having sex with a man. Nearby, there are a group of five drawings by Johann Hauser, all of them of grotesque naked women with wildly exaggerated breasts and genitalia facing the viewer, as if deliberately displaying themselves, their mouths and genitals wide open, their hair frenzied and massively overgrown. Counterposed with Hauser are a panel of six drawings by the Brazilian of Italian heritage Albino Braz. These are tightly controlled topless or naked bodies, men and women seen in positions dominant over animals or sexually with lovers. They all brandish a tool, a flower, or another animal. Whereas Hauser's work is scribbled and wildly drawn, Braz is mannered and executed with great care, possibly seeking likenesses in his figures. Even more proficiently and delicately drawn were the five works by Madame Favre that were discovered in a spiritualist's library in the 1930s. At first sight the finely drawn figures are very feminine, but on closer inspection a few are clearly trans sexual, with dark shaven complexions, of which one has a finely curling beard. Finally, in this section were the extraordinary, vibrant surreal works by the Lithuanian Friedrich Schröder-Sonnenstern. A giant-limbed, high-heeled, naked contortionist with a gaping vulva and two lightning bolts striking the ground from her anus; and a giant alien with two humanoid supporters descend on, and menace a small rural village There is something wonderful about these carnivalesque figures, suggestive of an unconstrained mind and wild imagination. To most visitors I imagined that this first volley of art brut was both strange *and* familiar. Strange in its explicit, detail, dress, times and gendering; but familiar in its deployment of many elements of folk and popular culture. A fearless, uninhibited, triumphant celebration of the body. A deployment of high energy, fecundity and exuberance; the possession of decontrolled, super powers and agency; gargantuan forms and excess; the capacity to change themselves and their worlds. The was the pan-European if not global popular culture of carnival surfacing in the work of people from all walks of life and nations.

There is something otherworldly and overwhelming about the carnivalesque art one encounters upon first entering CDLAB. There are no dull moments, nothing is ordinary. The works pulse and throb. One is aware that things are being revealed that are normally kept secret or private – or not even expressed. In this sense this collection generates an uncensored, highly charged emotional atmosphere, secret expression, exposure, revelation, shock, poignancy, sadness, anger. For the visitor, quite soon the everyday is suspended under the sheer force of this art. Yet, eventually we come to realise that they are *precisely* worldly and doggedly so. The images we see are profoundly connected to the way some people's lives and consciousness have been formed under a variety of shocking circumstances beyond their control, that are so extreme and painful, that so reverse/distort their normative cultural expectations, hopes, dreams and realities and are so pressing that they are forced into various forms of

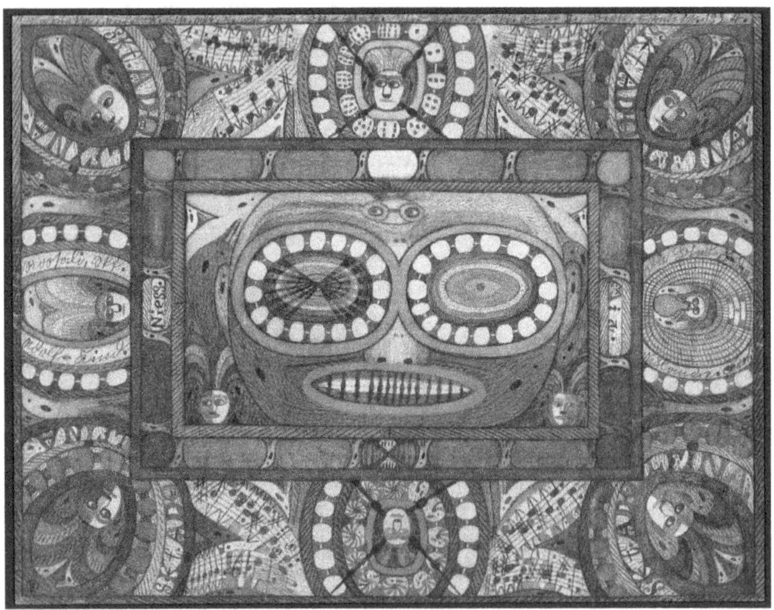

Figure 2.6 Adolf Wölfli, *Saint Adolf wearing glasses, between the two cities of giants, Niess and Mia*, 1924

negation, struggle and transition. This is what I wrote in my notes, what I grasped from my experience there.

The *3ème Biennale de l'Art Brut: Corps* continued on the second half of the ground floor and up into the first floor with the works of Aloise, Obata, Darger, Bartlett, Goetze, Jakic, Koczy, Nedjar and Podesta. However, such is the centrality of the body to much art brut that this exhibition bleeds seamlessly into other areas of the collection. Every so often there are extensive biographical notes on the artists/auteurs, which are more meaningful in their case than with professional artists since their expressive works are often directly related to their immediate life and experience, rather than to their quest for recognition in an academy – or to biographies of belonging to specific schools or styles. For the visitor to CDLAB therefore, the biographies can deepen an understanding of their art, or at least offer clues to their artists and the circumstances/sources of their creativity. The collection offers no interpretations of its own. And this deliberate policy allows visitors to forge their own.

In the case of a carved panel by Clément Fraisse (1901–1980), for example, it was astonishing how well his biography provided a means of accessing his expression and possible purpose. The carving was a large, beautiful and mysterious piece, a wooden wall panel measuring the exact length of the tiny psychiatric hospital solitary confinement cell it had been extracted from. Fraisse divided the wooden lining of the cell into a number of small panels into which he carved figures, flowers, wheels, animals and other objects.

When Fraisse (a native of the alpine region of Lozère, France) was about 30 years old, he was incarcerated in a psychiatric hospital, accused of attempting to set fire to his parents' farmhouse. Protesting his innocence loudly, he proved difficult to handle and for two years he was locked up in a narrow wood-lined cell with nothing but a chamber pot. Here was a man who had grown up on a family farm (among a family of 14 children) and had become a shepherd. It is hard to know how he coped with the transition from the open expanse of mountain valleys, alpine forests and meadows of his work to a life so spatially confined. All we know is that with the aid of a broken spoon, or, when confiscated, the handle of his chamber pot, he created a carved panel of great, if raw, beauty. While impossible to know exactly what he was trying to do with this carving, it is fairly clear that he populated his cell with other people, seemingly and teemingly, not repetitious copies of himself, but clearly different people from his life – his world. Around such people he carved elements of his alpine ecology and economy, sheepdogs, cats, narrow trees that were clearly pine trees, deciduous trees too; and beyond that across the vast swathe of the carving there were small circular symmetrical patterns with spoke-like structures that suggested alpine flowers such as the edelweiss that is especially native and common to this area (I checked this hunch later). To scale against these flowers, there were large wheels carved at the bottom of the panel ensemble, seemingly placed there as if one day they might propel his return back to this longed-for homeland. To me this artwork was also about loss and love, a world created to endure exile, a vehicle for the spirit of hope. I found his story cruel but triumphant. I was reminded of the significance of our material culture as repositories of identity, memory, belonging and sanity (Miller 2008).

When I finally obtained a copy of Peiry's book translated into English, and read her summation of visitor experience, I recognised the truth of it since I had encountered it myself, and seen it in the faces and body language of other visitors. She wrote:

> Textiles, statues and paintings are here restored to a setting much like the one in which they were first created – a place of shadows, secrecy and confinement. Everything seems to conspire here to ensure that the strangeness of the works combines with the feeling of disorientation experienced by the visitor. The discovery of the Collection de l'Art Brut thus becomes an intense intellectual and human experience producing what Michel Thévoz (1985) called 'the feeling of jubilation mixed with anguish and access to a still unexplored region of the distant inner self'.
>
> (Peiry 2001, p. 180)

I too saw people very emotionally absorbed in these works with faces held long in anguished concern, but where an occasional smile broke free. I had rarely seen this in an art museum before.

At the furthest end of the exhibition space, some visitors found the narrow strip behind the last series of works, in which were placed some chairs around two video monitors showing documentary film loops about Henry Darger, Sylvain Fusco, Masao Obata and Ataa Oko, among others. I think many people missed this feature, or found no seats available. This was a pity because here again, to persist and watch these was yet another way the research carried out by CDLAB had augmented visitor engagement and appreciation. Had these works been placed in the Centre Pompidou I was fairly sure that these films would not have been made, a point that vindicates Dubuffet's choice of Lausanne.

These films, made by curators at CDLAB, took the visitor into the homes, institutions and hospitals that featured in the life of these artists, and included some archival film, photos interspersed with interview footage with friends, family and psychiatric staff and in several cases the artist themselves. Without these it would have been very difficult to fully appreciate their works (not that this is essential, of course, or even possible in most cases), particularly since in many cases their works were not individual and separable but made in series, either developing narratives or repetitions around themes. To glean anything from a small selected number of Darger's works from the massive comic strip it belongs to, for example, would be practically impossible.

Masao Obata

The Japanese artist, Masao Obata (1943–2010) was filmed making his art and talking about it while working on his Kobe hospital bed (as he had always done) shortly before he died in 2010. It seems more than obvious that his parent's divorce when he was a young child had been deeply traumatising and scarring for him. After their divorce, he stayed with his mother and was raised by her and his grandmother. As a child, he liked to draw in secret, though we do not know what he drew. But we can guess. At the age of 30 his unsettled life was spent between time in psychiatric hospitals and a variety of temporary jobs. When his mother died, he went to live with his father but when he died soon afterwards, he became permanently installed in psychiatric hospital life. There, he resumed drawing – on large pieces of cardboard sourced from their kitchen. Working on his bed at night, he produced around one work per night, always stylised, carefully formed and decorated red figures, invariably of distinctive, happy (smiling) family groups: a husband and wife standing close together, often holding hands; often also with a little child between them and frequently a mother and a grandmother pictured together and with a child between them. They were drawn with a multitude of traditional outfits and (always) in idealised domestic settings. He frequently said the figures were his family, that he was the small child and that he missed them terribly. It is, of course, touching that through his drawing he brought his parents back together again, and allowed himself to resume being their loved child at around the age they divorced. He never pictured himself as an adult; he never grew up or grew old. Through his art he brought them into daily life with him in the present; in possibly the most unlikely setting for love to shine so prettily as it did in his drawings. Their clothes and rooms were garlanded with flowers and his mother wore jewels, and his father wore smart ties – and the family wore beautiful clothes, all of them created for them by Masao, as he worked on them through the night. Yet it was never overdone, the simple aesthetic of their domestic life as he still craved it was kept intact. They were all individually recreated perfectly intact, with their genitals always prominent (though never inflamed), and beautifully embellished.

Many of his works were thrown away before his art was discovered by contemporary artist Kaji Higashiyama who came in to lead weekly art classes at the hospital in 1995; after which many thousands were preserved (Maizels 2016, p. 168). They are both touching and stunning.

Henry Darger (1892–1973)

In the hands the American artist Henry Darger, we can see how art and creativity has been directed at a source of tyranny in his life. On first seeing the work of Henry Darger one wonders what could possibly lie behind its creation or its prolific and varied output; its depiction of 'unreal' times and landscapes of humanity populated by prepubescent intersex children engaged in a war with cruel adult forces. Darger's life story is also about sad and cruel loss, a child abandoned to the cruelty and heartlessness of adults and early twentieth-century institutions and psychiatry. His mother died shortly after childbirth when he was young and his newborn sister was quickly given up for adoption afterwards. He remained alone with his father until he was eight when his father's health problems worsened, and when, under the watchful eye of the Catholic church, his own behaviour was deemed abnormal. He was promptly placed in a Catholic boarding school for orphans. Later, he was sent to a faraway educational establishment for mentally handicapped children in Lincoln, Nebraska, where he stayed until he escaped, aged 17. Thereafter he lived quietly by day, working as a janitor in Catholic hospitals in Chicago, though by night his more serious and secret life's work was dedicated to the production of an ingeniously illustrated comic strip story of epic proportions: *The Story of the Vivian Girls in the Realm of the Unreal*, which ran to 15,000 pages. This work, alongside a biography and several other pieces of writing, were only found when he moved to a retirement home in 1972, aged 80. He died one year later. In my notes, I wrote: 'this is not art that reveals the condition of insanity, but art that describes and addresses the pain of cruelty, injustice and exile'.

Armed with just this version of his biography, visitors are inevitably inclined to interpret his art as resolving the trauma and injustice he felt during this life. In a comic book style, it tells of sisters (the seven Vivian Girls) empowered with beauty and strategic intelligence, who fight a long battle and eventually defeat an organised nation of evil adults who capture, incarcerate, torture and murder innocent children. A General Darger (clearly Henry Darger) is their adult helper, who makes strategic moves on their behalf and helps them out in numerous scrapes, though there are other benevolent Dargeresque characters who also assist them at critical junctures. Clearly then, it seems, Darger used his art to restore a protective connection to the last remaining member of his family who was lost and never found (his sister). Through his troubled life, we are to suppose, this art not only helped him to tell and realise a visually redemptive story, it allowed him to live in it, and shape it. As his long-time landlord Nathan Lerner, (a professional photographer) tells us:

> He didn't have any human relationships, not really. I did not know Henry for 20 years. I don't think anyone knew him. While he seemed a lonely man without friends during the day, at night when he entered his room, his loneliness must have vanished. He was in his own world of imagination, surrounded by all of his creations. He spoke to them [aloud] and they answered him [aloud, in different voices]. The room was small, but the world he created there had no boundaries.
>
> (Lerner 1987, pp. 4–7)

According to Faith Shields (2007) his early diagnosis as a feeble-minded child, and later his persistently disturbed behaviour and incarceration in a facility for the mentally ill, enable us, the viewing public, to understand Darger's complicity in this creative construction as entirely innocent, and yet also as heroic, admirable and original/authentic. This is a view shared by Maurice Thévoz (2001), Gary Fine (2003) and Richard Cardinal (2001) who all argue that its passion, self-involvement and compulsivity took the form of *possession*, a quality that was, for some, definitive of authentic art brut. Shields (2007) is less convinced: Darger was not so lost or mentally feeble.

As a result of the research carried out in the name of art brut, especially the analysis of his own written life history, Darger cannot be seen as entirely innocent. His devout Catholicism clearly mediated both his world view and his art (Shields 2007). MacGregor (2002) tells us that:

> … from childhood on, Darger was in conflict with God. He couldn't understand God's failure to answer prayers. His inability or refusal to prevent the sufferings of children, or to punish those who might harm them. Darger was tormented by God's evident silence in the face of evil. Throughout his life, his simple but profound belief caused him terrible anguish; often provoking him to rage, lived out in *The Realms of the Unreal.*
>
> (MacGregor 2002, p. 16)

In this sense, Darger's art also opened up a creative dialogue with his God in order to address his abandonment and the absence of divine intervention in his life and to strike back at him. But it is not hard to see that this art provided Darger with a world he wanted to be in and in which he could be an active participant, and engaged with the people in it. Shields reveals an episode in the story of the Vivian girls, where they discover a book and some pictures by a 'Henry J. Darger, author'. Weirdly for them, this tells of the war they are currently engaged in. In the following dialogue between the Vivian sisters, Darger gives away something of his purpose in writing this book within a book:

> 'Every picture seems to look you straight in the face as if you had some secret to tell them, or as if you suspected them of knowing your thoughts.'
>
> 'And probably he had them to use as company, as he was childless.'
>
> 'Maybe that is so, and he wanted them all to look as if they were paying attention to him,' said Jennie.
>
> (*Realms* Vol. One: 138 quoted in MacGregor 2002, pp. 20, 96)

Concluding discussion

In the absence of other channels for dialogue and expression, art is here available to these authors as a form of catharsis, hope and assertion, and perhaps justice and resolution of some kind. Art brut has been seen here as forming a parallel reality that offers a habitus and technologies of control for its artists/authors. Collectively their art therefore documents, narrates and confronts the human condition, in all of its manifestations and modalities and misfortunes. We see it secure another way of living for its authors but also an unintended means of communicating to us, its unlooked-for public. From being grounded in unreal lives, their art has worldly understandings and lessons to teach us. In the Lausanne Collection of art brut, one begins to sense their voice reaching out to us. Paradoxically, while their art has been removed from the contexts of its making, this anti-museum restores and preserves and honours the integrity of its maker's lives and art. Art is here connected to the communities that give rise to it.

One is tempted to agree with Dubuffet, that this art would not have had such support in the more limited aspirations and framings of art history, and nor would a visiting public have had the chance to explore it for themselves as they do in the Lausanne collection.

This art is also valuable in the sense that it is immersive and responsive to lives lived in many times and cultural spaces. From Dubuffet's initiation into Swiss forms of art brut, the collection now has a global scope. Its art has not been shaped into linear or progressive narratives, that support, extol or demonstrate the virtues of say modernity or nation, or culture or religion. It is necessarily non-linear and indifferent to ideology, though it may be located within struggles to assert or defend particular ideologies. It is necessarily *immanent* and therefore belongs to the possible worlds we create; it derives from them, and it is a part of them. Do we sense this as we trawl through this collection? Do we relate to it, sympathise with those who make it, experience empathy and sympathy and warmth? I think we do. And as a result, we leave with a feeling of not more or less cultural capital, but of having been emotionally engaged with its artists and their lives and circumstances in a much broader and possibly more valuable experience.

After 40 minutes or so, one realises that one has been plunged into something; it is in many senses the reverse of conventional museums: the problem is not so much in finding a way to engage as coping with the intensity of *so much* engagement, such a demanding, unremitting emotional ride. I was mentally quite exhausted after four hours, yet it was also as pleasurable and rewarding as a good film.

I could not say the same for my experience of Lille Métropole Museum of Modern, Contemporary and Outsider Art. While the Lille collection of art brut is strong and shares many of the same artists as CDLAB, it is displayed in a neutralising white cube setting and in a more open and sparse configuration, with the consequence that it is engulfed by the size of the gallery and lacks both emotional intensity or narrative integrity.

After spending two days in CDLAB one can make some tentative comments on its reception from visitors. People seemed to find it poignant: I picked up feelings of both tenderness and admiration for the artists and many of the works. The way the art is arranged alongside the narrative of its making and the often-secret lifeworld of the artist, provides a very personal (and privileged) connection between the visitor and the artist – a peep into their world that is normally unavailable. We can put ourselves in their shoes to such a sufficient extent that the connection is both objective and personal. Because *we feel* the churning emotion and experiences in their lives in a still vivid and fresh form, we feel some level of involvement and common humanity. We are not completely outside looking in. It might be outsider art, but it makes everyone appreciate the extent to which we are all outsiders, potentially. Insiders, only until further notice.

Their art also works on us, forces us to respond. It turns our thoughts to questions of uncaring cruelty and injustice; of barbaric 'treatment' regimes, past and present; it offers insights into mental ill health and its connections to individual biographies; it gives new angles on behaviour once thought depraved and unnatural; it warns of the dangers of societies that are not empathetic and loving. It underlines the precariousness of family and household in modern times and the senselessness of so many experiments to improve on tradition, or to make society more efficient.

At times, it is emotionally moving and hard going in CDLAB in a way it mostly isn't in conventional art museums. I felt the experience was very rewarding and I was surprised by this.

One risks generalisation, of course, but the extraordinary imagery, while always very personal and stylistically distinct, began to make a lot of sense in ways that it often does not in conventional museums of art, and here Lille was a telling comparator. At CDLAB one begins to form insights into art a little more deeply; the impulse to make it and the circumstances that prompt it being seemingly transcultural, though at the same time always culturally specific. The depth and breadth of the collection of CDLAB, both the extensive collection assembled by Dubuffet and the extensive later additions from further afield, also suggest the significance of temporal and cultural continuities and similitude.

One often feels locked out in white cube environments containing abstract modern and contemporary art, partly because the voice of the artist cannot be heard, but partly also because the art is self-referential, in a dialogue with itself (i.e. about the art world or art about art) to which we are mostly outsiders. At CDLAB the voice of the artist is clear and often anguished to the point where the viewer is curious to know more. Leaving visitors curious to know more is, for David Walsh, the owner-collector of Mona (see Chapter 5), a perfectly good objective for an anti-museum that seeks to extend art publics.

In the next chapter, we will encounter the American sculptor Donald Judd, another artist-founder of an anti-museum. Although driven to oppose conventional museums and the art world with a determination the equal of Dubuffet, we will see how he identified different objectives: to return art to the exact spaces of its making; to avoid fragmenting the oeuvre of great artists into too many anthology museums; to make museums the centre of art making and dialogue and to avoid spending money on flashy new architecture that is better spent on the development of art. Judd took his idea to a ghost town in an American desert wilderness and made it work.

3 Donald Judd's Marfa

State of dialogue

Donald Judd's anti-museum in Marfa, Texas, is about as far away from the conventional art world as it is possible to get – museologically and spatially. This was very much Donald Judd's intention. For Judd, the 1970s art world meant New York, and in his view it had failed and no longer served any great purpose. Conventional art museums certainly did not provide an adequate exhibitionary platform for the sculpture and installation art he was interested in (Judd 2016). In a grand gesture, he upped sticks and escaped to Marfa, a ghost town in the High Chihuahuan desert of Texas, near the Mexican border. Here, Judd 'created permanent installations of contemporary art that are among the largest and most beautiful in the world' (Smith 1994).

I flew in from Hobart, via Sydney, LA, and the desert town of El Paso. Marfa is a four-hour drive east of El Paso. On the final stretch of desert highway, a Prada shop, symbol of inner-city chic, comes into view. It's not a jet-lag induced mirage: it's the Prada Marfa. This is one of the most remote and deserted places on earth, even counting the low-key cattle ranching scattered among its mesquite, grass, yucca, cactus and tumbleweed ecology. Someone had the bright idea to build a small boutique-sized Prada shop art installation there and somehow it does not look out of place (it has fooled some shoplifters who have stolen handbags from its window). Surreally, the only people I saw on this desert highway were the art-world crowd that buzzed around it as I arrived and parked. I half expected to see trays of champagne and canapes circulating. Prada Marfa tells the weary traveller that they are nearing Judd's anti-museum, though this installation is by Michael Elmgreen and Ingar Dragset, two of the many great artists who have followed him to produce work there. Judd has built an extraordinary art complex in, and across, Marfa consisting of the Chinati Foundation and the Judd Foundation. Together they form a new kind of museum: 'or really an anti-museum. Judd figured out more than 30 years ago where American museums were going, and he marched the other way' (Kimmelman 2001).

Anti-museums USA

John Roberts (1997, p. 95) makes the point that the USA led the world in the making of anti-museums, after initially following in the footsteps of the Pompidou Centre, Paris. This was because the critique of the classic nineteenth-century modern museum and then the modern art museum was acted on most in the relatively stable, democratising political cultures of America between 1945 and 1980.

Up until 1945, more or less everywhere, the modern museum was a project of powerful nationalisms, at once a treasure house and an 'improving' educational establishment aimed at the working classes at leisure. Administrators and patrons oversaw this educative objective, believing that art would simultaneously civilise and tranquilise popular cultures tendencies to disorder and indiscipline. This museum model persisted until the second world war, after which there was an upsurge of working class expectations, democratic expansion, increasing consumption of art by a rapidly growing middle class and a dramatic growth in new art schools – where the new politics met contemporary art. Museums could no longer merely extol the virtues of past bourgeois achievement and had to respond to the arrival of a new and modern era (Roberts 1997, pp. 94–95).

Initially, it was especially in the USA that an 'opening up' of museum culture was most pronounced, through the building of a new era of modern art museums, beginning with Lloyd Wright's Guggenheim in New York (1943–1959). Roberts (1997) argues that while some curators did embrace art as a living dynamic of modernity, releasing art's power to usher in social change, the dominant curatorial response was to 'aestheticise a formal version of it', and to suspend it in an emotionally sterile white cube environment, as if it had been especially designed for this environment. It was a benign, passive and conservative aesthetic of the modern era, little better than the closed museum it replaced. In the USA, artists increasingly rejected both the white cube as championed by the Museum of Modern Art (MoMA) and MoMA's suspiciously close ties with corporate America (Lorente 2011).

> The US-led version of the modern museum, as yet another space of disinterested contemplation, began to unravel when a crisis in modernist architecture met this crisis in modern art in the early 1970s. The purity of the museums exterior and interior was seen as an authoritarian extension of the narrow definition of what counts for culture on its walls. The Pompidou Centre in Paris, swept this to one side in favour of architectural diversity, of multiple use, of expanded subjectivities and aesthetic traditions, of anti-elitist education, of popular entertainment, of gallery walls and café tables.
>
> (Roberts 1997, pp. 94–95)

The spirit of the Pompidou Centre, if not its excessive, expensive architecture, took root most strongly and sustainably in the USA. The black liberation movement, feminism, environmentalism and the alternative society movements, the American Avant Garde (and others) of the 1970s were such that they provided a continuous and relatively coherent pressure to diversify and produce new cultural institutions and exhibitionary platforms for contemporary art (Smith 2009, 2012; Roberts 2015; Phillips 2017). Architectural preferences for reusing abandoned industrial buildings in out-of-the-way places came to replace commissions for contemporary architecture in central cultural precincts. Here was art expressing its dislike of capital and its increasing spatial separation (Ley 2003). New York was going to become a hive of new exhibitionary platforms in quirky spaces and places. The modern sculptor Donald Judd would move out of New York to do something revolutionary.

Donald Judd

Donald Judd's art practice and strongly expressed opinions were also formed within the twin crises of modern art and modern architecture, and the art museum's resulting loss of cultural authority among artists. Judd felt that art had become merely an excuse to build more architecture. To him the vast sums being spent on buildings that should have been spent on growing art had become an entrenched feature of the art world (Judd 2016).

In the early 1970s, Judd's art making, art practice and exhibitionary principles co-evolved as a work in progress, brought together in Marfa as he built, first his home, studios and installation spaces at the Mansana de Chinati (aka *The Block*), and later, the Chinati Foundation, in collaboration with Dia art foundation, on a deserted US Cavalry base on the western edge of Marfa. His day job as an art critic, once necessary to makes ends meet, now focussed and sharpened his thinking on the relationship between art and museums of art. As Stockebrand (2010, p. 13) reminds us, the focus on a few artists and their installations that we encounter in the middle of a wilderness today strikes the visitor as inevitable, but it took Judd a long time to work out and execute this concept, from his trial permanent installations in Spring St, New York, in 1968, and throughout his time at Marfa. Through the experience of having seen his own and so much other good work exhibited badly, he asked himself, at the point of expanding his operation considerably, how it might be done better.

Unusually, at Marfa Judd was dealt a good hand: limitless financial backing from Dia's access to an oil fortune, endless space, cheap abandoned buildings of every form and complete autonomy to experiment with a new vision. Judd's Marfa then was the result of a very specific conjuncture, and a tightly interlocking set of personal circumstances, character and luck. It was as rare as it was potent. It would become an art oasis in the desert and one of the art worlds most treasured places. It would inspire new art and forms of exhibition globally.

Before moving to Marfa, Judd had already begun to assemble his work in permanent installations at his Spring St studios, New York. These would lead him to push for permanent installations for his work and that of others, as he believed that temporary exhibitions, being designed by curators for the public, placed the art itself in the background, and ultimately degraded it. For Marianne Stockebrand, his curator and long-time partner at Marfa, the overarching project 'sprang from the desire to create a new form of museum, one that moved beyond ordinary collecting criteria and instead came under the aegis of the producer, i.e. the artist himself' (Stockebrand 2010, p. 13). Here again, we have the artist and art itself as the proper subject of the anti-museum.

As he was preparing his installation and living space at Marfa, he was also 'forging clarity' through his writing (Stockebrand 2010, p. 18). His

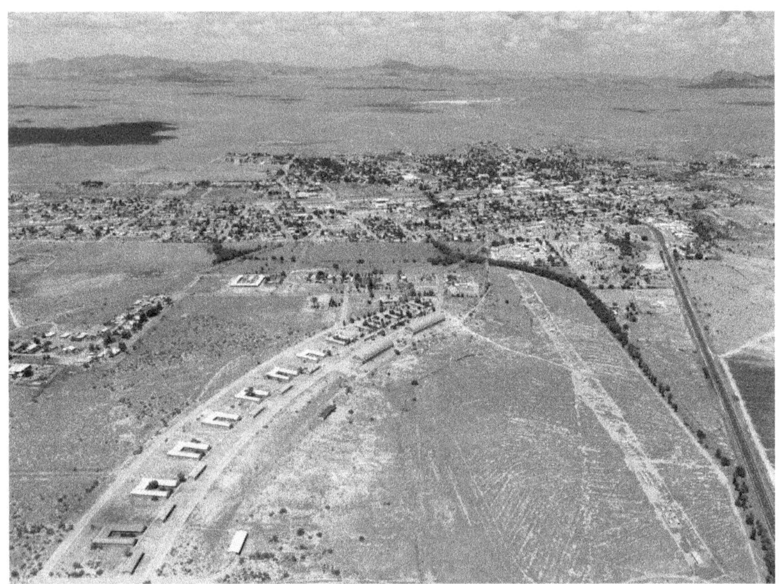

Figure 3.1 Aerial view of the Chinati Foundation, courtesy of the Chinati Foundation

Photo by David Keller, 2018

1973 essay called 'Complaints: Part I', for example, is probably his most considered and thorough critique of art museums (Judd 1973); here is the kernel of his argument:

1. Installations in museums are too crowded and make little effort to realise the requirements of the artworks themselves.
2. Painting and sculptures are currently exhibited together in such ways that neither can be properly viewed. No notice is taken of their specific types of spatial needs and this degrades the work and the curation.
3. The exhibition scene has to change: there should be fewer exhibitions and they should be more carefully prepared.
4. Art is frequently damaged through careless handling during shipment. Insurers, shippers and handlers have no respect for the works. How can we subject our most important art to a life on the road that is disrespectful and damaging? Further, it is unsustainable.
5. Art rather than art history should be a museum's first consideration; they should support and promote the production of art and the artists; 'museums of contemporary art are there for the present'.
6. 'There is a unity between art and the place in which it is created' and this should be preserved in some way and reflected in where it is exhibited.
7. Individual artists should be collected in depth: 'there should be rooms somewhere or small museums where a portion [of their work] is visible and permanent' (Judd 1973, p. 209) – otherwise they become scattered by the art world and viewed out of context, or in misleading contexts. Pollock's work, for example, is intimately connected to the New York of its making, yet this unity has been dissected and dissolved into anthologies of art everywhere. In a later working of these ideas, the 1982 essay called 'On Installation', Judd wrote: 'A museum is the collection of an institution and it's an anthology. A few anthologies are all right, but some hundred in the United States alone is ridiculous. It's freshman English forever and never no more no literature' (Judd 2016, p. 311).
8. A disproportionate amount of money goes into building museums to the detriment of the collections.
9. 'A relatively small number of visual artists, themselves insufficiently supported, are supporting by what they do, a large superstructure of museums, and curators, art departments, and art teachers, critics, some art historians, some architects, money dispensers, some commercial art and so, on' (Judd 1973, p. 207).
10. Museums and collectors favour small-format works over large works as easier to transport and sell; museums are not adequately equipped to present larger works.

11 Art should not be judged solely by commercial considerations and art and its exhibitionary institutions require more sources of funding, private as well as public.

Judd was not against all art museums. Some such as The Metropolitan Museum and the Frick Collection were praised. However, Judd was thinking beyond conventional museums as inevitable places for supporting, displaying and encountering art, and in many ways, he wanted to dissolve the museum as an art institution separable from art's making and makers, its contexts, its reception and discussion – and to bring artists and their public closer together.

> … he found it strange to replace art with art history, arguing that only what is created at a specific time and place can be regarded as 'our' art and culture – that is, the art and culture of the present. Judd considered a lively dialogue among artists and their works to be more meaningful than the clinical dissection of first-rate artworks. His writing from these years convey the strong desire to live in such a state of dialogue and to participate in it as actively as possible.
>
> (Stockebrand 2010, p. 14)

Making the Mansana de Chinati (aka The Block)

Born in Excelsior Springs, near Kansas, Missouri, in 1928, Judd's first taste of the true West came in 1946 as he moved through US 90 as a US soldier on his way to post-war Korean operations. In a telegram to his mother he noted the beautiful country and mountains around Marfa. He came back to the southwest on family holidays during the late 1960s, to Arizona, New Mexico, Baja California, now on the lookout for a place to find a house as a bridgehead for a planned escape from New York. He thought Arizona too crowded and New Mexico too high, but then he remembered West Texas. This was high desert rangeland with mountains in every direction; it was sparsely populated and, as he put it, 'the land was undamaged' (Judd 2016, p. 427). In 1971 he moved to a rented house, Casa Lujan, on the eastern edge of Marfa and then rented a storage building. Judd drove a truck full of art from NY to store there. In 1972 the family stayed for the summer at the house and in 1973 he bought two former aircraft hangers that had been moved onto the same central city block. In 1974 he bought the rest of the block, which included a smaller two storey office of the former Fort Quartermaster. Altogether, this was a huge yet compact arrangement.

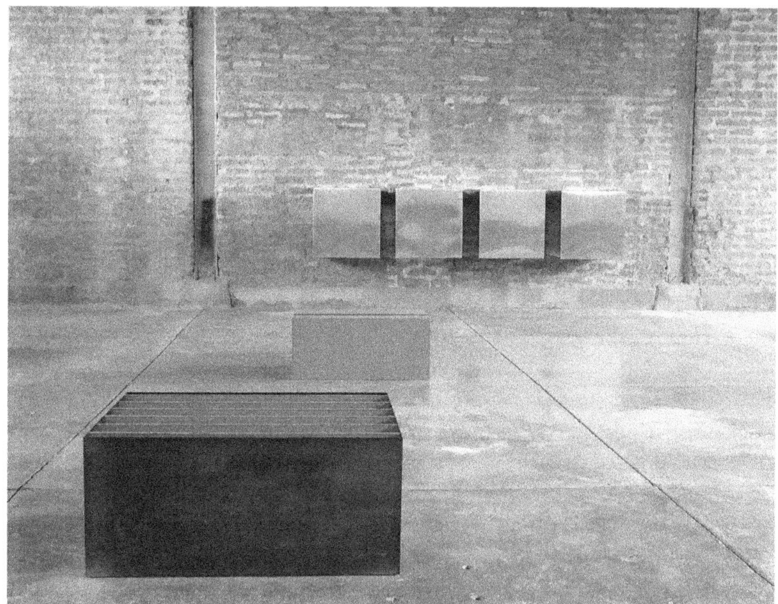

Figure 3.2 South room, west building, La Mansana de Chinati/The Block, Marfa, Texas

Over the next few years these uninhabitable buildings on 'The Block' were brought into service. The east building was prepared to install art in one section and by 1976 he had built a kitchen and a bedroom on the other side. Then a studio was built in the west building followed by a new installation room (with his art in it) and a narrow (though large) library. At the same time, he had a team of workers building an adobe wall around the entire block, and an inner adobe wall on the highway side to provide sound proofing. Finally, the two-storey house was brought into use, consisting of 'two children's rooms and the necessary domesticity', as he put it (Judd 2016, p. 429). The block was completed with two smaller adobe buildings, a bathhouse and an office, alongside a vegetable garden, a chicken house, a pergola and a pool.

The making of Dia Art Foundation, Marfa, and the Chinati Foundation, Marfa

On the 18 April 1978 Judd met with Heiner Friedrich and Philippa Pellizzi, who, with Helen Winkler, had founded Dia (an art foundation whose aim was to support 'those works of art which cannot obtain sponsorship or support from commercial and private sources because of their nature or scale', Stockebrand 2010, p. 31), and they were especially keen to commission artworks for specific places, both indoors and outdoors (Urbaschek 2003; Stockebrand 2010, p. 32). They agreed to create 'a larger awareness of Donald Judd' and particularly the work he intended to do in Marfa, which was going to be large, unsupported by other means, and both indoor and outdoor installations. So, while many rightly see Judd as the inspiration and driver of Marfa's transformation to a major art world site, 'his fusing of art, architecture and environment' (Yarinsky 2011), the concept of even doing so in such a place, in such a manner and on such a scale was an artefact of the vision of the three Dia founders, and their access to the substantial funds from the Schlumberger oil fortune (Philippa Pellizzi was the daughter of John de Menil and Heiner Friedrich was her husband and successful art dealer (Wilsey & Beal 2012; Yarinsky 2011).

The original idea was to produce a permanent installation of Judd's large sculptures, both existing and new, Marfa-made works, in a Marfa warehouse, of which there were several disused contenders in and around the town. Originally the intention was not to produce a museum at all, merely to install large works in an apt building (Stockebrand 2010, p. 31). However, as time went by the project was scaled-up considerably, in part because other artists were added to the project and in part because of spatial opportunity: there was simply a large supply of very cheap buildings available in Marfa. This prompted the possibility of including artists whose works resonated with Judd's and each other's. Hence Marfa became a place where other artists came to work, and leave their work there, permanently. The first of these were John Chamberlain and Dan Flavin who Judd admired, and whose large works chimed well with his (Judd 2016).

In October 1978, Dia acquired artillery sheds (built 1939) in the grounds of the decommissioned Fort D.A. Russell, on the southwestern edge of Marfa. A perfectly pleasant walk or cycle ride from La Mansana. Then, they purchased a warehouse of the former Marfa Wool and Mohair Company in the town centre. The initial idea was to permanently install large works by Judd, Chamberlain and Flavin, some of them to be created on site. The outside and inside art works were duly commissioned and Judd was given huge scope to shape and manage the restoration of the buildings, the installation of the art and artistic decisions. For this he was given a Dia salary. Meanwhile, Dia was going to establish an administrative and curatorial office to take ownership and management of the art works and ultimately to organise visits from the public. They thought the building and the installation would take five years.

In 1979, Dia acquired a large proportion of the other buildings in Fort D.A. Russell – notably, 11 U-shaped barrack blocks (which can be clearly seen in the foreground of the aerial photo on p. **000**), the Arena, swimming pool and sundry small buildings plus their Ice Plant in Marfa – providing a total land package of around 340 acres, and some 40 buildings. This was now on the scale of the biggest art establishment anywhere and Judd set about building his legacy with great vigour. His project management of these buildings, all of them at varying points in their transformation, was formidable (Shafer 2017).

During the 1980s, the buildings and the grounds were cleaned up and restored to a high spec while retaining their original style and feel. Judd set about designing and commissioning the manufacture of 15 large concrete works that would eventually span the length of land between the Fort's buildings and the US 90 highway. Then, the two massive artillery buildings were re-roofed and given new glass windows with desert views. At first, one was to house a Commission of 50 large Judd works in mill aluminium and in the other, Chamberlain's Texas Pieces of large works (crushed and mangled cars). In the event, Judd made 100 aluminium pieces and they occupied both buildings, to stunning effect, while Chamberlain's installation was moved into town at the Marfa Wool and Mohair Company building and John Chamberlain was given the Ice Plant for his studio. The Chamberlain Building was inaugurated in 1983.

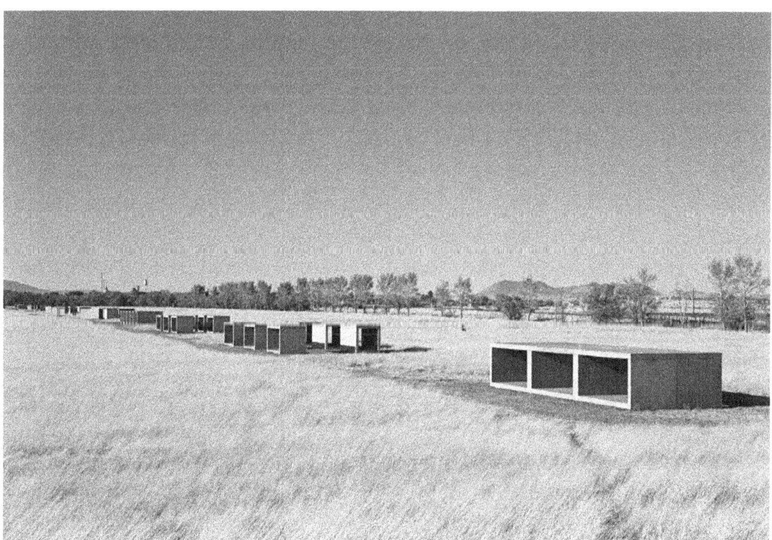

Figure 3.3 Donald Judd, 15 untitled works in concrete, 1980–1984

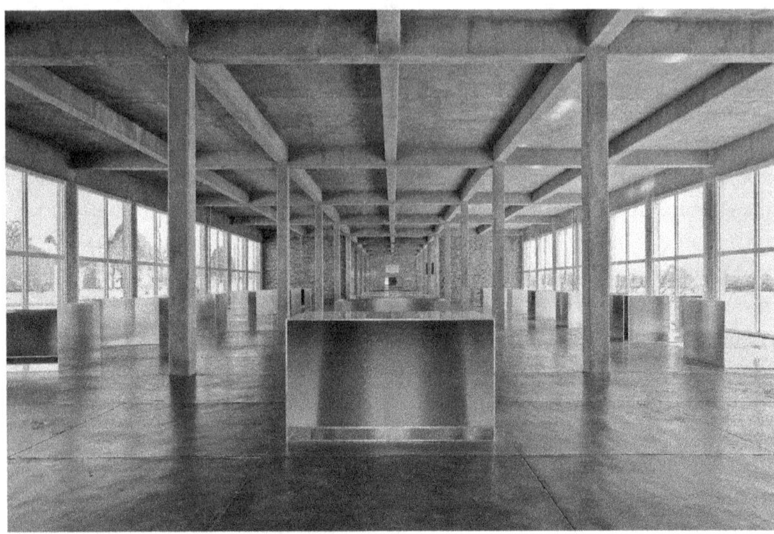

Figure 3.4 Donald Judd, 100 untitled works in mill aluminium, 1982–1986. Permanent collection, the Chinati Foundation, Marfa, Texas

Photo by Douglas Tuck, courtesy of the Chinati Foundation. Donald Judd Art © 2017 Judd Foundation/Artists Rights Society (ARS), New York

But then disaster struck their source of funding in the form of rapidly declining stock prices of Pellizi's Schlumberger Oil holdings. The Marfa Project was halted and renamed *The Art Museum of the Pecos*, with Judd one of three trustees. Dia had to divest itself of its plans, sell off art works from other projects and set up a not-for profit art foundation to take over what they had begun in Marfa. This was a heavy blow to Judd because he had been expecting Dia to carry on with the administration of the project. In 1986, the art, land and buildings owned by Dia were transferred as a massive grant to the new Chinati Foundation, with Judd as Director and responsible for its project management and completion – which Dia agreed to pay for in the form of a five-year transitional funding agreement. How it could be financed after that was an open question and a huge concern.

The first catalogue of the Chinati Foundation was designed and written by Judd in 1987 in order to celebrate the opening of the new entity as well as the installations for himself and John Chamberlain and the massive party space of the newly completed Arena where the celebration would be held. The Arena was a core social space that has continued to hold major art world events, openings and local gatherings – with a scale and versatility for gatherings that few other museums possess. Summing up what had so far been achieved in Marfa, Judd wrote that the Chinati Foundation:

> .... is now one of the largest visible installations of contemporary art in the world, visible not in storage. When it nears completion, or even now, if my own complex [i.e. The Mansana] is added, it is the largest, as befits Texas
>
> (Stockebrand 2010, p. 35)

Rob Weiner arrived in 1989 as an assistant to Judd and from his conversation with Kathleen Shafer it is possible to see how Chinati, the Judd Foundation and the bringing of Marfa back to life was a very hard fought battle with the desert and a deserted town that had been almost completely destroyed by a 1950's drought.

Around the time Judd's *Mill Aluminium* pieces were first installed, Weiner described the atmosphere and art scene emerging in Marfa as 'exciting' (Shafer 2017, pp. 128–129). 'We were so occupied with what we were doing that you didn't take time to feel deprived. It was much tougher then because there wasn't much activity at all, and the main streets were boarded over ...' (Shafer 2017, pp. 128–129). But it was changing for the better: 'Artists were coming. It was already for me an intoxicating situation'. It was drawing in a significant amount of interest from artists globally, through the events Judd set in train, and Weiner confirms something that has remained true ever since. Marfa's attraction was not merely because of its collection of curated artist's works, it was a living, gathering and creating place for artists too and one that is constantly enriched for visitor's experience by their *presence.* They continually *add* to it, want their art to be there, and give their art freely to it. They became a critical part of civic life in the depopulated town and gave it an artistic tone that other visitors could be a part of, especially in its nightlife. This is a completely different experience of art from conventional art museums. This texture and richness was well captured during the documented 2012 visit of Sean Wilsey and Daphne Beal for *Vanity Fair*.

Although he never wished to build an anthology museum, it is fairly clear that he had begun to see the need to add more works, especially large outdoor works, the works by other significant artists that he had collected, as well as an increasing number of gifts from visiting artists. Richard Long and Roni Horn were added in 1988; Claus Oldenburg and Coosje van Bruggen in 1991; Ingolfur Arnarsson in 1992; Ilya Kabakov and John Wesley in 1993.

After Donald Judd

In autumn 1993 Judd was diagnosed with non-Hodgkinson's lymphoma. He died in February the following year, though many of the things he had set in motion continued to roll on and enrich both the Chinati Foundation and the Judd Foundation, which was also set up to maintain his own New York and Marfa buildings and installations. In 2000, when Chinati finally opened Dan Flavin's *untitled (Marfa Project)* in six of its barrack blocks, the original decision to install Judd and Flavin together in the same setting was vindicated. According to Marianne Stockebrand (2010, p. 37): 'as soon as the lights were switched on, ablaze with pink and green, blue and yellow light, their bright artificiality and opulent sensuality suddenly seemed the perfect juxtaposition to Judd's aluminium works just a stone's throw away'.

Other works have trickled onto the scene steadily and seem set to continue doing so, in part owing to Judd's extensive contacts and friendships in the art world and in part to Chinati's energy generated through its extensive network of internships, visiting artists, openings, October Open Days and the normal hum and throb of Marfa's permanently passing-through international art community. It is also true that Judd's former assistant and partner, Marianne Stockebrand, was skilful and dedicated in making sure Chinati did not go under, in part by mobilising Judd's dedicated admirers. Carl Andre came soon after Judd passed away in 1995; David Rabinowitch was added in 2007; Robert Irwin's *Apache* arrived in 2016 – and, in fact, Irwin has moved to Marfa and is planning on converting a derelict Marfa hospital into a major land art piece that showcases the local desert landscape. The Judd–Marfa show rolls on.

Wilsey and Beal remind us that for a long while after Judd's death (the Dia transitional funding ran out in 1991 and the museum was left just $400 on Judd's death), the place fell into mourning and a standstill. Curators were not paid, no visitors came to the town and it was deserted once more. Stockbrande rallied Judd's famous art friends as noted above, but what made Marfa was the channelling of Judd's idea of dialogue and inclusiveness:

> Chinati also supported up-and-coming work. In the case of [Jeff] Elrod, Weiner's endorsement brought him to the attention of the New York art dealer Pat Hearn, who sent down a truck and filled it with every painting the artist had made during the last six months of his Chinati residency. She sold the lot in two weeks, transforming his career. Chinati was always, as Weiner puts it now, 'watering the culture of the place. We had to make sure that each person who came

> was enchanted by it.' And so: internship and artist-in-residence programs, free children's art classes, lectures, banquets, concerts, and symposiums such as 'Art and the Landscape' and 'Art and Architecture' (bringing in architects such as Frank Gehry and Jacques Herzog). Weiner and Stockebrand also continued Judd's tradition of annual open-house weekends with music, a barbecue for the whole town, a bonfire, and offering the use of empty exhibition space for pretty much any local artist or performer with an idea.
>
> (Wilsey & Beal 2012)

In the aftermath of Judd's earthly presence came journalists and writers who, like Wilsey and Beal (who visited in 1996 and 2012), were seduced by their journey to Marfa as much as they were entranced by what they found there. As it got written about, its notoriety as edgy, different, hip and cool and at times a little mad – a story about a place that unswervingly refused to sell out to the art world – so the visitors came. Their numbers increased, as word spread about its easy going, low-key, bohemian culture (Wilsey & Beal 2012), and the two Foundations were championed as a special kind of museum by artists themselves. In turn, Jeff Elrod's studio became a major evening hang-out for artists of every hue and visitors alike. The legendary walk-through installation *Hello Meth Lab in the Sun* created in 2008, by New York installation artist Justin Lowe (with Jonah Freeman and Alexandre Singh) is widely regarded as one of Marfa's best creations, but Lowe told Wilsey and Beal that 'By the end it felt like the whole town had contributed in one way or another' (Wilsey & Beal 2012). The point where the various Foundations and studios end and the town begins has now become beguilingly blurred. Such a significant, unplannable state of dialogue surely stands as one of the greatest art achievements.

Visiting Judd's Marfa

Without Dia's continuing patronage, the Chinati Foundation needed to secure its funding on a firmer and permanent footing. Part of that involved securing a flow of money coming in from public visitation. The creation of the Chinati Foundation, based largely at former Fort D.A. Russell, did not include those properties that Judd had acquired for the purposes of living, working and the installation of his earlier work, as well as his extensive collections of art, objects, furniture, his paintings, prints and architectural drawings. Some of this was contained in his Mansana de Chinati or 'The Block' as it was known. However, between 1988 and 1992 Judd acquired for himself, a lot of other buildings in the Downtown area to the west of Highland Avenue and there his collections were carefully curated into particular themes, and aspects of his art practice and studio operation. These included a former Bank (The Marfa National Bank), a residential building, a supermarket, a hotel, and other commercial buildings. All of these buildings were part of Judd's Estate and they were folded into one entity, *The Judd Foundation*, controlled by his executors, Flavin and Rainer Judd.

To survive, both the Chinati and Judd Foundations had to create a flow of income from visitors and in this they both have a strong, if separate, interest. By 2011 Rob Weiner estimated that there were 11,000 visitors to Chinati, a significant increase from the 5,000 arriving in 1995 (Shafer 2017, p. 128).

The Judd Foundation lacks the operational budget to keep a museum open to the public, so instead they offer guided tours and use a variety of interns and other local artists to guide them. This is another way of funding emerging artist practice. Judd Foundation offers two different guided visits of their properties in downtown Marfa, those to La Mansana de Chinati/ The Block, and those to rest, collectively known as 'The Studios'. Typically, they offer up to two daily tours of The Block and one tour of the Studios and charge $25 per head for each (although entrance is free for residents of surrounding Presidio, Brewster and Jeff Davis Counties).

The Chinati Foundation is open to the public Wednesday through Sunday, 9am to 5pm. Visitors have a number of options. They can self-guide themselves around specific artworks on the Fort Russell complex: e.g. to walk around Judd's perimeter concrete works is free, while $10 is charged for each of self-guided tours of Dan Flavin's light works, Donald Judd's *Mill Aluminium* and Robert Irwin's *untitled* (*dawn to dusk*). Guided tours are offered to the complete collection (a 4.5–5-hour marathon, with an hour's lunch break in the middle), or a Selections tour to the founding artists work: Judd, Chamberlain, Flavin and Irwin (a shorter 2.5-hour tour).

It is thus always possible to experience all of Judd's achievements (and those of his Foundations) over the course of two days, so that a very intense weekend is offered at Marfa.

I wanted to experience the intensive tour and stay in Marfa for a typical stay. I arrived in Marfa on the 7 April 2018 and left on the 9th. I planned to start with a Studio Tour before seeing The Block, thinking that I would gain a broader and deeper sense of Judd through his workplaces and collections from his life before Marfa. Then, it made sense to see how, at The Block, he made a new life for himself and his family in Marfa, and began to identify a methodology for permanent installation of his work as well as designing and reshaping buildings for this setting. After that, I would tour Chianti Foundation, the crowning glory.

Studios Tour

The tour group numbered some 15 people, noticeably a youngish crowd with a few older couples and the odd aging sole parent with older children. They all looked like museum-goers, they were notably international, and most were working in the cultural economy and/or collectors of some kind. There were Brits, Belgians, Italians, Dutch, Spanish, Canadians, New Yorkers and Californians. I walked up from the Judd Foundation Office with the guide to the start of the tour at Art Studios, in a former supermarket building. Laid out inside were the wooden benches on which were received newly made Judd art works from his manufactures, alongside some of the pieces themselves and the tools and equipment of the installation process. We were immediately pitched into the heart of the Judd operation at Marfa alongside the bewildering range of objects required for Judd's anti-museum work. It was a colourful and design-filled space – full of shapes and colours from the 1970s and 1980s. In conventional museums, the tools of museum work and the transitional stages of making and exhibition are rarely seen, but from this experience I could see how interesting it was to visitors and how it connects visitors to the art and the museum.

We had the briefest of introductions, more or less telling us what the room was used for and that the room had been left exactly as it was found

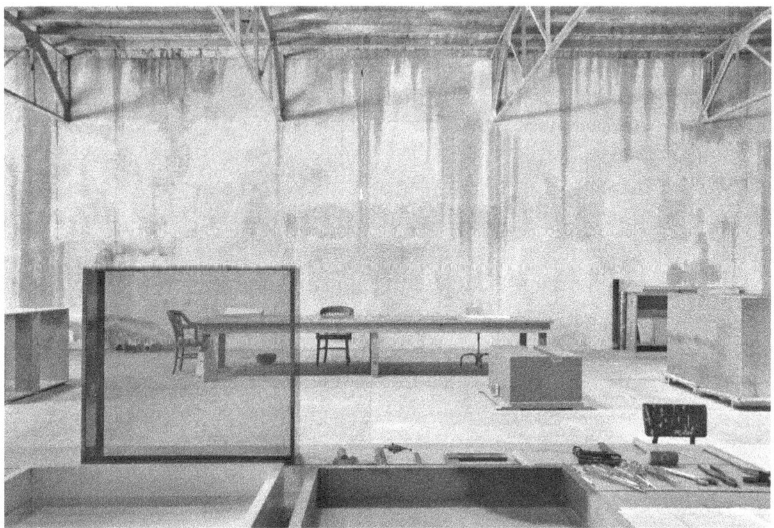

Figure 3.5 Art Studio, Marfa, Texas

Image: © Elizabeth Felicella, courtesy Judd Foundation, Donald Judd Art © Judd Foundation

on the day Judd died. We were then left to walk around the space until we had finished looking at everything. Only when we were all ready to move on did the guide intervene, and even then, it was only to take questions. In keeping with Judd philosophy, it became clear over this and other tours that wall labels, explanatory boards or human tour guides were not to mediate any contact with the art, the space or the objects. We were to use our eyes and think for ourselves.

Further along the same street, on the corner with the main street of Marfa was a large and imposing bank building in Spanish Revival style. In the spacious ground floor was a collection of early Judd paintings and possibly some that he painted in Marfa or for this building. As a group, we were still very much a mute body, keeping our thoughts to ourselves, but I felt we were wondering about each other and watchful. On upper floors, we came across Judd's collection of modern furniture (1940s–1950s especially) as well as some of his own furniture and architectural designs, in the same sparse, pared-back style (Van de Rohe, Aalto, Schindler, Reitveld etc.). Judd favoured those with his own aesthetic: 'open planar construction and geometrical simplicity' (Fones 1996). These spaces were beautifully filled and it proved too much for some, especially those who shared his aesthetic and collecting enthusiasm: suddenly, spontaneous emotion, appreciation and discussion broke out, and from there on, we were a noisy and opinionated group that the tour guide was going to find difficult to keep to schedule. I noticed that people ventured beyond the subject matter immediately at hand, and began talking about themselves. Within a short time I became knowledgeable about their work and careers, how art and life configured in their own home spaces, why they liked Judd or what they liked and did not like, and some details of where they were staying and how they came to Marfa.

We then went to the Whyte Building, a soft and easy-going weatherboard bungalow at the back of the bank, with nice proportions, in a small garden. In 1991, Judd selected this for some of his early 1960s paintings in combination with a set of seductive Schindler furniture, everything beautifully positioned in otherwise stripped-back rooms. Light poured in from its French windows, the interior tones and textures tracking the sun. It was a stunning installation. We coveted the Schindler pieces with hungry eyes.

We then visited several smaller, former residential buildings and other commercial buildings full of Judd's very distinctive 1970s–1980s style, and by the time we had viewed these building we had a good sense of his character and aesthetic sensibility/reach. These buildings were afterthoughts, after his primary public work at Fort Russell and the Block had been completed. This was Donald Judd at home, backstage, something done for himself. Seeing the potential of these small-town buildings for art installation encouraged others to buy into Marfa and add to its art-rich cultural ecology. Indeed, several other art foundations moved to Marfa after Judd, notably Ballroom Marfa, 'a contemporary cultural arts space that presents a variety of visual arts, film, music, and performance programs by emerging and recognized artists, while maintaining a strong connection to its community through such efforts as community dinners' (National Endowment for the Arts 2019). This 'remote clustering' continues today and gives visitors a unique opportunity to experience the potential for museums to connect informally to living art worlds and cultural terroirs around them; a night-time counterpoint to the 'Judd' Foundations' formal presentation of self.

La Mansana de Chinati (The Block)

We met our guide at 4.30 pm at the front gate, a smart, clean Judd design exactly at the midpoint of The Block's considerable stretch of El Paso Street. A dozen of us entered and sat at the large wooden table under a pergola. It had been a hot day and its cool shade was a welcome relief. We listened to a general introduction to Judd's history in Marfa, since not everyone had been on a tour previously, and then to a potted guide to the contents of The Block, consisting of three significant buildings, an impressive adobe wall structure, a pool, a garden, a forecourt, a chicken enclosure and a dog house.

Because the guiding policy was largely to show and not tell (apart from responding to questions at the end of each segment), a significant amount of time was again spent being on our own at each of the tour stop settings. This was the home of a renowned artist who died 26 years ago, who was fresh in our memory, and whose private quarters we were now crowding into. His home was also left perfectly intact on the day he died, and our intimacy with it was marked by solemn silence. At certain points, especially arriving into the set piece installation spaces of Judd's work in the east and west buildings, there were some gasps of awe and appreciation, and many couples gave each other knowing smiles. At no point, did we break into freeform conversation or pleasantries. To judge from looks, behaviour and the kinds of questions that were asked, this group were mainly art world types, most of whom worked in the cultural sector.

Some people were clearly significant fans of Judd. They would check angles and distances, look at works from different places and find pleasing juxtapositions. Points of entry, that Judd considered important for the viewing of his work, were especially well-worn locations for contemplation. Aside from the set piece installations of Judd's sculpture, there were collection spaces, for textiles, pottery, cookware, books and document showcases on benches and objects randomly placed. Some of these were in functional domestic spaces (the kitchen areas, sleeping areas, sitting spaces, studies), though for Judd it seemed that all spaces were seen as aesthetic spaces and everything seemed very carefully placed within them. Judd *was* somewhat obsessive about this (Serota 2004). But here we understood why he raged against museums, that removed art from its life. We were engaged with a home where everything was a display of different kinds and where the line between 'art' and the everyday, the sacred and the profane was blurred, or the distinction rejected or ignored. Beds, for example, were seen in studios, installation spaces, the library as well as bedrooms. This was the idea of an anti-museum realised with exacting detail; taken to its fullest extent.

Chinati Foundation

The Chinati Foundation has a smart office/ bookshop building just off the car park in Cavalry Drive. The guide was a bright, sparky character who was currently an intern of the Chinati Foundation. We, a group of some 12–15 people, moved under the veranda of the office building to hear his introduction, rules and housekeeping, and an excellent potted history of the Judd transformation of Fort D.A. Russell. We were already armed with good maps of the site so everyone was comfortable with what would turn out to be a full and complicated day. Outside, beyond the office were the two, huge former artillery sheds and beyond them, desert as far as the eye could see. Even the nearby US 90 was lost in the desert scrub. This group gelled very quickly, partly I think because we had a lot in common. There were a group of costume dressers from Hollywood; there were artists; there was a New York fashion designer; there were a couple of architects from San Antonio; a few cultural academics; and various museum, design and art world people.

Moving first to Judd's *Mill Aluminium* installations, we paused before going in to hear the 'dos and don'ts' (no photography, no touching the art, etc.) and some basic facts about what was inside the two buildings. However, during the oration most of us had turned our heads to take in a small herd of deer that walked nonchalantly into shot, unseen by the guide. It was almost comic. The first question after the guide had finished was therefore: what were they and, could we please take photos of them? Stealing the show were indigenous pronghorn deer, apparently the second fastest land animal, after the cheetah. They are commonly seen around Chinati but are not fed or encouraged by staff there. They are simply part of the landscape; it is a wilderness landscape right up to the Chinati buildings.

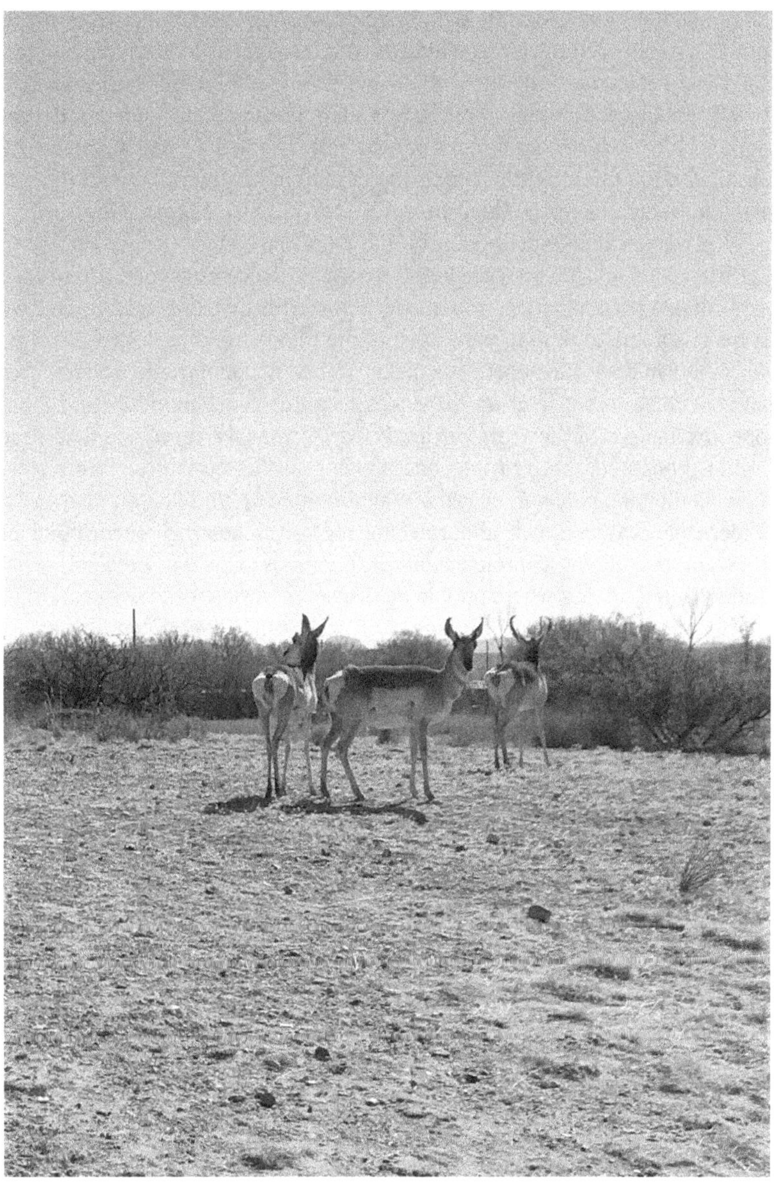

Figure 3.6 Pronghorn deer at Fort Russell, Marfa, Texas

Photo courtesy Tamra Collins

During our long spell among Judd's *100 Mill Aluminium* pieces, we all kept mostly to ourselves. Judd had stripped out the former hangar doors to put in floor-to-ceiling glass windows that brought the desert and desert light right into the building. I think we were spell-bound by the strange beauty of the aluminium cuboids and their juxtaposition with the desert, and unable to form anything we especially wanted to say to complete strangers. Engulfed by the desert, the ensemble of shining, unearthly perfection seemed like something from Kubrick's *2001: A Space Odyssey*.

We were equally spellbound by the Dan Flavin light works set out in six barrack blocks that curved along the arc of the campus road. Combined with the Judd installation, this made a powerful first impression, and we were given lots of time to view each of the Flavin buildings. As we waited for others in downtimes between them, we had the opportunity to idle, chat and socialise. From then on there was laughter, more intimacy and more open exchanges of views on the art. After 90 minutes, it seemed that these initial groups had blurred into one another so that now, group conversations could take place on occasions, again, often around the art, so that the experience was as much about seeing the art as hearing others point of view, or exchanging comments and observations. This was precisely what Judd wanted. Places where art can be discussed; a state of dialogue.

By the time we were looking at Roni Horn, Claes Oldernburg and Coosje van Bruggen, John Wesley Ingolfur Arnarsson and Robert Irwin and others, we had turned full circle in that these were more like group or collective viewings, where discussion between visitors was as likely the medium of engagement as individual contemplation. The art conjured multiple subjectivities, favourable and unfavourable comparisons, delight, anger, frustration, awe, scorn.

Judd did not like art history or instruction getting in the way of the people attempting to look at art'. In 1983, Judd wrote: 'So far I've not wanted to explain my work since the work is intelligible and explanations should be unnecessary and are always somewhat *deforming*' (Judd 2016, p. 321, my emphasis).

Anti-museum Marfa style

As we have seen, separately or combined, the Judd and Chinati Foundations are anti-museums in the truest sense of the word. From Judd's own writings, (which are unusual in documenting very fully the various interventions he made across an entire career), he explicitly designed and executed a new form of exhibitionary platform that opposed what he considered to be the fatally flawed nature of generic art museums and their exhibitionary strategies. In his view these undermined and deformed both artists and their art, and in order to address these flaws Judd set out to recreate them anew as art- and artist-centred entities, to allow artists to take over the role of installation and curation, to remove didacticism as their centrally organisational aim and to remove art from the harmful influences of the art market, corporate power, and party politics – and possibly also the widespread conservatism of museum professions. Nothing would ever be perfect, but this was something at a time when most art museums were doing very little to address long standing criticisms. And, unlike conventional museums that are structured by widely agreed upon aims, values and museological practice, Judd's anti-museum vision was uninterested in merely replacing them with another set of immutable museological practices. His anti-museology was responsive to artist, place, ecology, space, time, contexts and the reflexivity and subjectivities of a viewing public.

The next chapter shows two anti-museum variants that attempted very similar transformations. While remaining in New York, PS1 and the New Museum created art museums in out of the way areas normally ignored, or avoided, by conventional art museums. And while they foregrounded artists and brought artmaking into their museums, these were projects by curators rather than artists. New Museum focussed its energy on the art making and exhibition of emerging contemporary artists rather than the established artists that were prevalent at Judd's Marfa. At the same time, the New Museum focussed especially on building a strong exhibitionary platform for women's contemporary art, and supporting a body of artists who had struggled, with little success, to obtain gender and racial equality in conventional art museums.

4 New York, New York

PS1 and the New Museum

Introduction

The best way to encounter the New Museum, New York, is by walking east along Prince Street, Soho, to the junction with the Bowery. Boutique eateries and fashion stores occupy the old buildings along Prince Street, but this cosy, gentrified strip, once the immediate neighbourhood of David Bowie, intersects jarringly with a scruffy section of the Bowery, where every other store sells wholesale kitchen and catering equipment. These stores occupy the ground floors of what were once nineteenth century factories and warehouses and the Bowery retains elements of its former skid row status, including hotels for the homeless and down-and-outs. Rising above everything on this inauspicious junction is the luminous 2007-built, eight-story, New Museum building by Tokyo-based SANAA, a striking pile of white rectangular and square blocks with one of the best views of Manhattan looking north from its rooftop Skyroom. Somehow SANAA made a pile of bricks seem soothing. It's a good start.

That said, as I crossed the road to go enter at 10 am, a man in soiled clothes was rather nonchalantly pissing on the central reservation. Was it one of their performance artists or a local – hard to tell around there these days.

This solid, clearly art-world building, crashing in on the Bowery's genteel poverty, is the one case study that looks, from the outside, to be most like a conventional white cube art museum. But, behind the plan to build it was a deliberate policy to scale up what had always been its exciting anti-museum intervention on the New York and international art scene (Gladstone 2012). It has strong roots in the 1970s/1980s New York alternative art space phenomenon, and perhaps has remained the most true to its activist origins as an art institution determined to oppose the conventional character of an art museum.

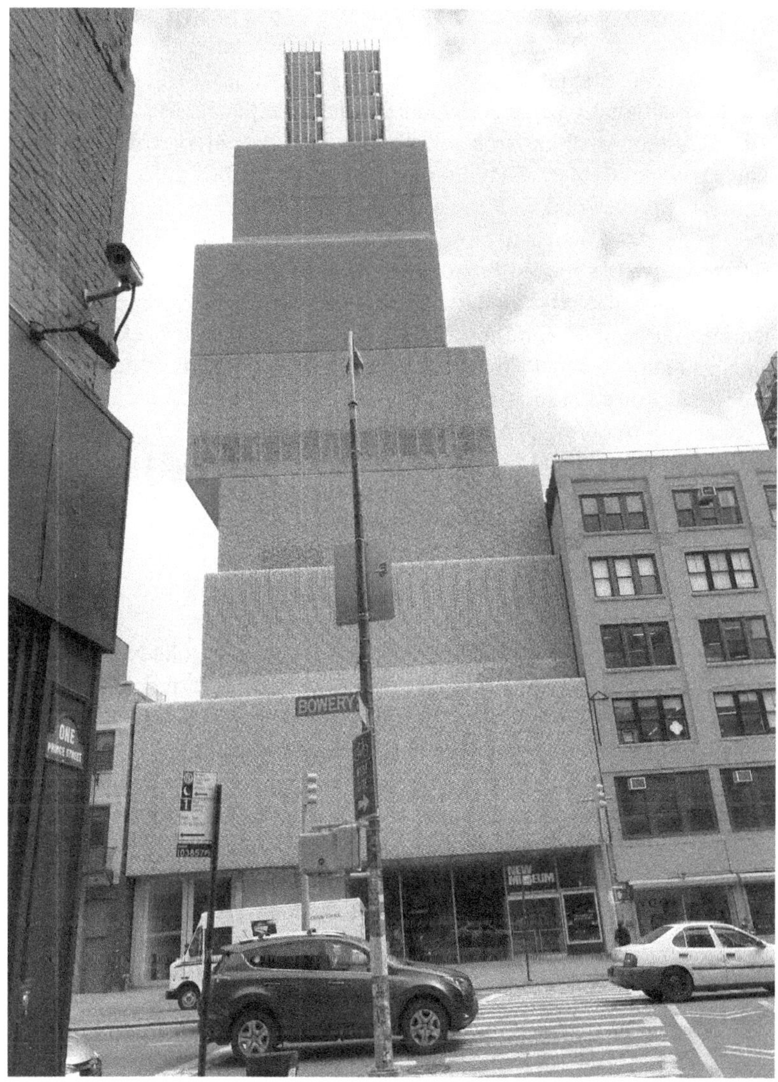

Figure 4.1 New Museum, façade on Bowery taken from Prince St

Photo: Adrian Franklin

As its current Director, Lisa Philips has argued, when the New Museum was founded by Marcia Tucker in 1977, it 'was one of a crop of alternative spaces that sprang up during the 1970s … an explosive phenomenon that changed the artistic landscape of our country' (Phillips 2017, p. 10).

These alternative spaces included: The Alternative Museum, Artists Space, Anthology Film Archives, the Clocktower Gallery, Creative Time, The Drawing Center, Film Forum, 98, Green Street, Idea Warehouse, Apple, C Space, Franklin Furnace, Just Above Midtown, the Kitchen, PS1, the Public Art Fund and more. And, as Phillips notes, 'many of these enterprises were founded by and/or run by women who faced barriers to advancement in conventional organisations and were emboldened by the feminist movement' (Phillips 2017, p. 11). Thus, Marcia Tucker was one among many women, including Alanna Heiss (PS1), Martha Beck (Drawing Room), Linda Goode Bryant (Just Above Midtown), Karen Cooper (Film Forum), Anita Contini (Creative Time), Martha Wilson (Franklin Furnace) and Helene Winer (Artists Space) who forged 'alternative structures that endured as a vital counterpoint to mainstream institutions', at least until recently (Phillips 2017, pp. 11–12). Marcia Tucker said that their leadership of alternative museums meant they were marginalised 'by virtue of having had to create the institution in order to work in it' (Phillips 2017). It was a price they were happy to pay.

Among the most long-lived of these was PS1, which, like New Museum is still very much in business. However, in 2000 PS1 merged with the Museum of Modern Art (MoMA) to become PS1 MoMA. MoMA, the archetype of convention it had opposed so vociferously.

While Alannah Heiss herself devised this merger in order to set PS1 on a firmer financial footing, and told M.H. Miller (2016) that it 'anesthetized some of its wildness', one has to wonder whether the influence flowed the other way too. Whether by 2000, MoMA's twentieth century iteration had run its course and was more than happy to take a walk on the wild side. By 2000, modern art was being eclipsed by a new form of contemporary art (and artist) that was a lot less easy to domesticate neatly in standardised white cubes and modernist narratives. If Adrian Piper's show *A Synthesis of Intuitions: 1965–2016* (2017) at MoMA was anything to go by, its stiff, formal and uncontroversial character has been loosened, if not entirely liberated, on the top floor: for example, while I visited recently, a largely white audience were dancing along to Piper's funk dance class performance piece, *Funk Lessons (1983*) (Piper 1983). It is instructive to think that *Funk Lessons* was first shown at *The Alternative Museum*, New York, in 1983, and would never have been considered at MoMA at the time.

As still vibrant and true to their values, and still influencing artists, curators and museums, MoMA PS1 and the New Museum are very significant, especially since, as Miller says, alternative art spaces have all but disappeared in New York (Miller 2016). The Alternative Museum itself was founded in 1975 and closed in 2000.

How and why PS1 and the New Museum became established by two women, Alannah Heiss and Marcia Tucker, reveals some important, and distinctive circumstances contributing to anti-museum thinking in the 1970s. Heiss's PS1 was established one year before Tucker's New Museum, in 1976, and a brief account of her story provides the context that also enables Tucker's contribution to come into focus. While the specific conjuncture of the art world ecology in 1970s New York did provide common possibilities and patterns among these leaders of its alternative art spaces, there was enormous latitude for these individuals to depart from, and oppose, museum norms in centrifugal and varied ways. After convention is dropped, many new things become possible.

Alannah Heiss – Founder and Director of PS1

Born in Kentucky and raised in Jacksonville, Illinois, Heiss was a graduate of the Lawrence Conservatory of Music. In 1971, she set up The Institute for Art and Urban Resources (with Brendan Gill), a New York organisation dedicated to bringing into use, empty or abandoned buildings in order to produce or display contemporary art (Clocktower 2014). Some 11 properties were used at various times. The 1971 show/event *Under The Brooklyn Bridge*, which included some early appearances of Sol Lewitt, Carl Andre and Gordon Matta-Clark, was an instant success. In 1972 she set out to establish a more permanent gallery set-up, culminating in the iconic Clocktower Gallery on a Lower Manhattan corner building owned by New York City Council. This provided exhibitionary opportunities for many emerging artists including Marina Abramovic, Gordon Matta-Clark, Vito Acconci, Carl Andre, Gordon Matta-Clark and Laurie Anderson, among many others.

A successful small gallery and connections with the key circle of New York contemporary artists made Heiss more ambitious. Still working under the umbrella of her Institute for Art and Urban Resources, she began to seek out a permanent large space, though a modest budget meant she was still in the business of taking on derelict buildings in odd, out of the way places. (Miller 2016). With only the promise of a $100,000 grant from New York City Council of the Arts and a $100,000 bank loan, she viewed various possibilities from Staten Island to Fort Apache, but decided that a former Romanesque-revival, 'double sized' public school building in Queens, Long Island (also owned by New York City Council), near the transport hub of Court Square was ideal. PS1 opened in June 1976 (PS1 meaning Public School One).

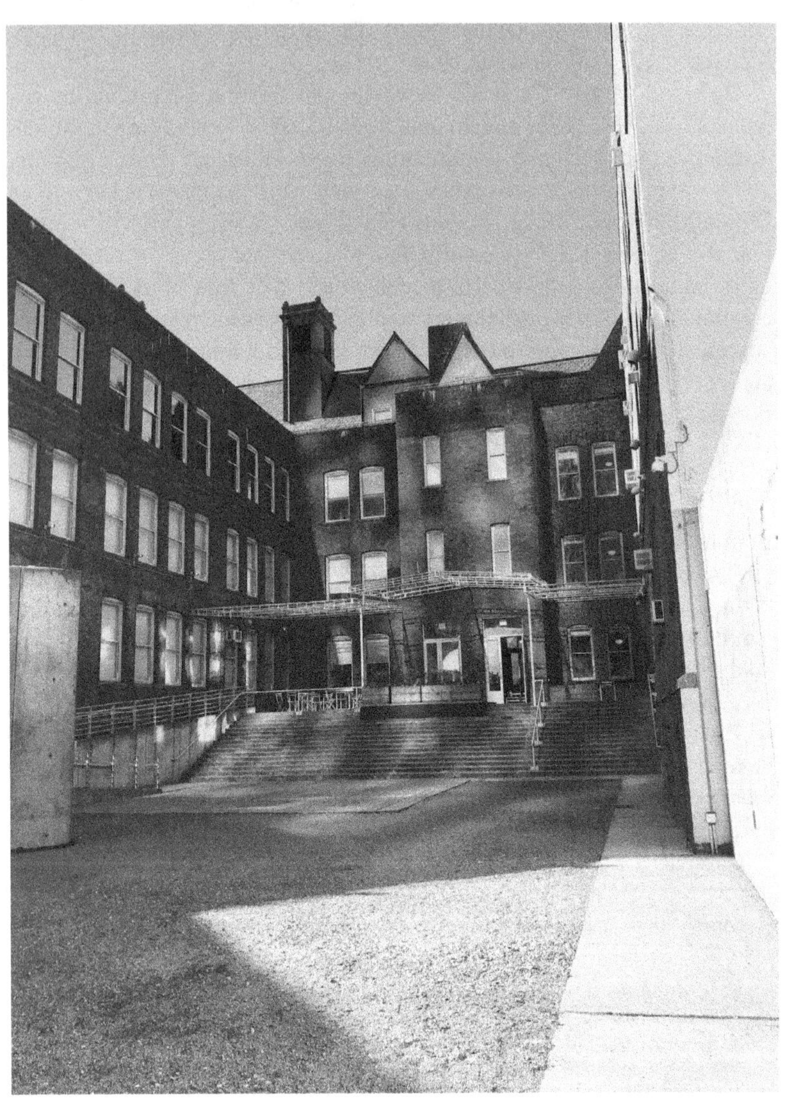

Figure 4.2 PS1 building

Photo: Adrian Franklin

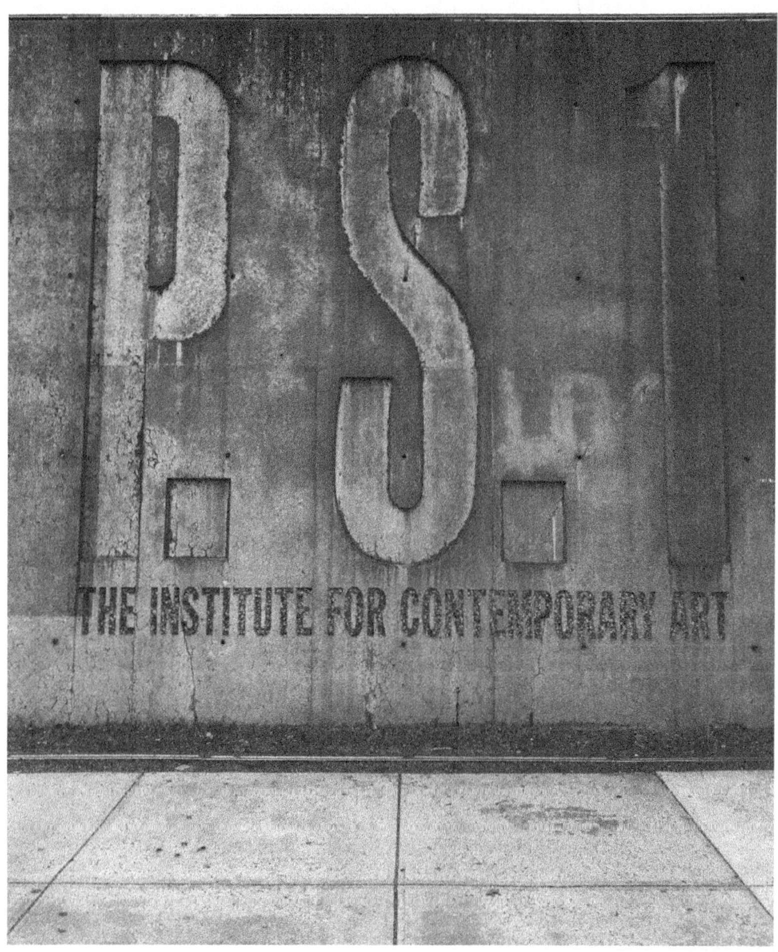

Figure 4.3 PS1 entrance sign

Photo: Adrian Franklin

What drove Heiss to struggle with crumbling buildings and insert artists and their art in the poorest art-free neighbourhoods of New York? She told H.M. Miller (2016) that she saw museums as a problem. Collections should be accessible on-demand, more artists of her generation should be taken seriously, and she was especially interested in providing better spaces for sculpture and installations than most museums did. She felt she should develop a different kind of museum, as an example of what an alternative *museum* institute might become – the notion of something 'fixed' being less appealing than something that evolved. It came to be an exploratory, dynamic, experimental place of site-specific art, and open to all artists not merely to exhibit there, but to participate creatively in its life.

> I decided to give up on my little spaces all over. They were guerrilla efforts, and I wanted [instead] to be a grown-up radical. A grown-up radical starts her, or his, own thing and sees it through, takes the criticism from other radicals and tries to solve problems instead of marching. I had wings and a halo – everything I needed – so I decided to build an anti-museum. That's what P.S.1 was. It had nothing to do with alternative spaces. It didn't have anything to do with galleries, and nothing to do with helping poor artists, like Artists Space. The last thing in the world I would do was not show an artist because she already had a gallery. I wanted to have the strength of New York artists and the dominant artists in the world....
>
> (Miller 2016)

Looking back at their beginnings on the occasion of the opening of their Dance Pavilion and 2nd season of Warm Up (in 1999), Heiss said, 'P.S.1's mission has always been to provide opportunities for both emerging and established artists to execute projects that might not be possible anywhere else'. She told Miller: 'I tried to adjust whatever was the prevailing mood or temperature of the outside world, to see what we could do that would open up another door' (Miller 2016).

One door that opened derived from the relative flexibility and novelty of the spaces that her buildings provided. The state of decay, the absence of purpose-built galleries and the proliferation of small and quirky spaces in PS1 provided a 'built-in' opposition to the mainstream art gallery, which also then shaped very different museological, curatorial and display cultures. It forced curators, more often in conjunction with artists themselves, to use the building as part of the thing exhibited, and not as a neutral container. As star curator Massimiliano Gioni told Andy Battaglia (2017): 'At P.S. 1, the space itself was so present and so radical that you couldn't just borrow some painting and put it on the wall. It was more about making environments'.

This is illustrated by its formative first exhibition, *Rooms*, where in June 1976, 78 artists created site-specific installations (each in a former classroom) at a time when the building was still in many senses derelict.

> The show is now legendary – a remarkable sampling of contemporary art from the mid-'70s and probably the pinnacle of site-specific installation, with each work created for its sublimely decrepit context. Gordon Matta-Clark removed portions of the floors from the first, second, and third levels of the building, converting the old school into a massive sculpture of negative space. Alan Saret carved a hole into a wall on the third floor, which was designed to focus a beam of light from outside into the building, and it still exists today. The show positioned young artists, who had received little to no attention from American museums on the frontlines of the avant-garde, and helped make Heiss into a folk hero in the process.
>
> (Miller 2016)

Works by Richard Serra, Cecily Brown, Robert Turrell, Pipilotti Rist and Sol Lewitt are among many long-term site-specific installations still at PS1. It never settled on a formula but remained energetic, innovative, experimental and opportunistic, always-already to respond and adapt to their external ecology at local, national and international levels. PS1 liked to give good artists good exposure and that meant working hard on building a bigger audience for contemporary art (Heiss 2012).

Heiss told Battaglia (2017):

> That's what we all are: show makers – not collectors, not gallerists. You start asking yourself, 'Why do you do this show or that show?' You do it not to prove a social welfare point or an exclusionary point, but because you're looking around and saying, 'What is it that people need to see, where is the hole in what they're not seeing? What has not been at MoMA, the Guggenheim, the Whitney?' ... With 130 rooms from 1976 on, we were able to show not just every artist in the world but every artist who thought they were an artist, everybody who went to school in art.

In the early days PS1 was also a hothouse for artists themselves. Not just to exhibit but to be given studio space to make art within the site – and then to exhibit it – and this was being done on some scale, through national and international schemes involving partner sponsors in the home localities and nations of the artists. That way, PS1 was organising some 200 to 300 shows a year, giving over a single room at a time to a rotating list of curators, who would present small exhibitions in short bursts. This meant that the museum was refreshed frequently and this encouraged habitual repeat visits from across New York and beyond. In this way, PS1 kept pace with, or perhaps set the pace for the rhythm of New York's fast moving contemporary art scenes – illustrating at the same time how slowly (if at all) the conventional art museums responded to the same pace.

Heiss was also willing to entertain, and to 'up' the expectations of an art going public. As a musically trained person, it is not surprising that music featured in her anti-museum thinking. What is a little more surprising is that the nightclub became a stronger influence than the museum.

> Most museums now host live music and events to appeal to wider audiences, but Heiss ran hers as a centerpiece of her programming, much as a media or performance department might function today. For a long time, Heiss said, PS1 was the only nonprofit member of the New York Nightlife Association.... One of PS1's longstanding advisors was Rudolf (no last name), the club owner who ran some of New York's historic venues – including Palladium, Danceteria, and the Tunnel. As the institution aged, during the '90s Heiss would often come to Rudolf with concerns about keeping PS1 relevant as it became more and more entrenched in the city's art scene.
>
> (Miller 2016)

But the new ideas kept coming. Former playgrounds around the school provided a substantial space for art, gatherings or both. *Warm-Up* was unleashed in 1997 as a summer-long dance party designed to bring new audiences to PS1 and Long Island City, Queens. From July to September PS1 became a regular weekend music + art venue and hangout for New Yorkers. *Warm-Up*, was a series of early evening concerts that created a bridge between groups of families and friends and leading edge musicians, prominent DJs and contemporary art. Music, which was more popular and accessible, became in this way, a pathway into the less known field of contemporary art. The indoor gallery spaces were kept open and audiences were encouraged to check out the art while music played. In this way, Heiss avoided creating an easier, dumbed down art experience for non-gallery goers. She told Miller: 'I don't want to change the work that I show. I don't mind P.S.1 being seductive for non-museum audiences, but I don't want it to form shows for that audience' (Miller 2016). At the same time, she was adding serious musical links to the art: 'we were treating DJs very seriously, treating them like artists'. The list of musicians was very impressive, including: DJ Harvey, Groove Collective, Afrika Bambaataa, Mad Professor, Richie Hawtin, François K, Fischerspooner, Kid Koala, Arto Lindsay, Scissor Sisters, Luke Vibert, Solange, Jamie xx, Grimes, Arca, Black Dice, Four Tet, DJ Premier, Derrick May, Venus X, Mattis With, Naomi Zeichner, Dean Bein, Matt Werth, Starchild + The New Romantic, Discwoman and DJ Kass. Building on this was their concurrent outdoor film festival, which took place in the courtyard at dusk on Thursday evenings (July through September). In other words, PS1 became a hangout, a place to inhabit rather than visit occasionally, part of the cultural habitus of city dwellers.

Visiting PS1

On a quiet week day morning in December 2018, I visited PS1 during Bruce Nauman's *Disappearing Acts* show. The building was busy and the café full at lunchtime. I was interested to know whether their 1999 merger with MoMA had changed the feel of the place, some ten years later.

The settled, understated and hip character that Heiss established is still there. Its informality, absence of glamour and minimal security still makes this an unhurried and relatively low-key experience where visitors may still become aware of themselves in a disused school building that has only recently been taken over by artists. Much of the school's nineteenth-century institutional harshness remains: the steel mesh covered stairs, the sparse polished linoleum corridors, the featureless interior. It's the complete opposite of art world glitz and more like a nineteenth-century hospital or asylum. Against this backcloth, the art is vivid and still a surprise to find in all its spaces, nooks and crannies. Despite having a major renovation in 1995–1997, with a new entrance, outside event spaces and enlarged gallery spaces, it still feels abandoned, desolate and unloved. Heiss did not want the building to be gutted, or made pristine. The architects were told 'to expose the bones of the 100,000-square-foot space' (Louie 1997), which they did without giving it any semblance of loft-living chic. This was a grim building and it still is, but in many ways, it is a more fitting environment for much of the thoughtful, socially critical contemporary art it has shown than the pure white cube it avoids – the white cube, which aims for neutrality but fails because its empty, spotless vastness in an expensive postcode only ever evokes the power of the super-rich. By comparison, PS1 sits comfortably within its scruffy bit of Queens, and no doubt the sound of rappers and DJs emanating from its courtyard on long summer nights interpolates locals as much as anyone.

Marcia Tucker – founder and director of New Museum 1977–1999

Alannah Heiss wasn't the first, or the only woman to be an anti-museum thinker in New York. She is notable because she did something about it that is unique and has stuck. Her alternative art space, PS1, is still with us, even if it is now holding hands with big MoMA, the matriarch of all conventional art museums; and even if the merger with MoMA has 'anesthetized some of its wildness' as Heiss claimed (Miller 2016).

Marcia Tucker is notable because she created an anti-museum *museum* that has avoided convention, did not stifle wildness and has encouraged it consistently. But it was also an overtly political activist space that sought to increase diversity and equality in the art world and deploy art and its political charge in order to activate cities and communities – in its immediate neighbourhoods and globally. New Museum and PS1 are monumental achievements, still great assets for New York. The New Museum has not been taken over by a conventional art museum behemoth.

In the introduction, I argued that 'the wonder is not that there are anti-museums but why there are so few'. One answer is that while those working inside conventional art museums have often been keen to change them, in line with the full force of the anti-museum critique, conventional museums themselves are largely very *resistant* to anything like the fundamental change involved (Lorente 2011; Prior 2002). Marcia Tucker's story illustrates this perfectly. Conventional art museums are overdetermined by an academic art history (and its professional monopoly of curatorial labour markets) which, its critics say, limits visitor engagement and the transformational capacities of contemporary art, as much as it hampers doing anything significant about their built-in problems of taxonomy, chronology and repetition (Green 2018; see Tucker in Phillips et al. 2019; Judd 1973). While claiming to be change orientated, in recent years the curatorial profession clings passionately to their traditional priorities and their expertise and change little beyond 'heightened participation' and commercialisation (Hanquinet & Savage 2012; Radywyl et al. 2011). They maintain didacticism, or what Hanquinet and Savage (2012) call 'educative leisure' over social transformation as their main role and 'take-home' for visitors, while their connections to incumbent power is tangible, operational, financial and ideological (Bennett 1995; Marr 2008; Rentschler 2015). In recent years, under regimes of ever-diminishing public funding they have also thrown in their lot with urban redevelopers and conservative city councils seeking the illusive Bilbao Effect, a strategy long associated with the dangers that gentrification poses to local artists, cultural terroir and poorer residents (Ley 2003; Zukin 1995; 2010; Shaw & Porter 2009; Rich &

Tsitsos 2016; Ganning 2016; Matthews 2014; Sasajima 2016; Schuetz 2014). In many ways, their (largely ineffective) civilising mission, begun in the nineteenth century, has barely changed anything significantly (Bennett 1995; Franklin & Papastergiadis 2017). The rich, educated and privileged still dominate art, the art world and gallery -going; they still make strangers of the working classes (Prior 2002).

For Alison Green, contemporary art culture is increasingly and inextricably linked to social and political issues: 'the museum … needs to be radically reimagined for a renewed public purpose. Contemporary art's presence in it is, within this framework, the disruptive thing that destabilizes museums' (Green 2018, pp. 104–105). Unlike many in the alternative art space movement, Marcia Tucker pioneered the notion that there might still be room for the necessary reform within a museum format itself, and set about experimenting and demonstrating its potential in a determined, single-handed and open-minded way – often using powerful contemporary art to do precisely this (Battaglia 2017).

It was while doing *just this* as a young curator in the late 1960s and early 1970s, that she tested the tolerance limits of the conventional Whitney Museum of American Art where she worked. She curated shows by vociferous American women artists; 'daring group exhibitions' by emerging contemporary and performance artists including the infamous *Anti-Illusion:Procedure/Materials* of 1969 (which drew extremely critical reviews from the likes of Cindy Nemser in *Art Education*) and a survey show by Richard Tuttle. She also championed radical forms of art-making such as tattooing 'that many considered outside the boundaries of art' (Phillips 2017, pp. 7–8). An incoming Director in 1974 sensed that their core values (educative leisure) were under attack. Tucker was fired in 1976.

Apart from defending educative leisure, the New York art scene was also in the thrall of politics and powerful lobbying groups as the reaction to the much-anticipated arrival of Charles Saatchi's *Sensation* to the Brooklyn Museum (October 1999 to April 2000) demonstrated. The hit exhibition of Saatchi's collection of YBAs (young British artists) was immediately attacked by establishment forces. One of its works, Chris Ofili's *The Holy Virgin Mary* (1996), which used elephant dung to form one of the Virgin's breasts, and tiny collaged pornographic images falling like snowflakes around her, created a storm of protest among Christian religious groups. As a result, the Mayor of New York City, Rudolph Giuliani, removed its $7 million city funding. The House of Representatives also passed a non-binding vote to remove their federal funding. Subsequently, after heated competition to win Sensations for the Art Gallery of Australia, it was cancelled there too.

As these examples show, from the 1970s to 2000 it remained very easy to overstep the mark as a young curator inspired by a new generation of contemporary art. Or, put another way, it was becoming increasingly difficult to work with emerging contemporary art in conventional art museums funded from government sources.

In her reflective essay [originally a lecture given in 2003] 'Why Art Matters' (2019), Tucker argued that '... one sure fire way of resisting change is to work from our successes rather than our failures. An artist friend told me that a virtuoso looks at where they've been rather than where they are going ...' (p. 240). She thought curators were no different:

> ... my motto was 'Act first, think later' – that way you'll have something to think about. That could be a recipe for disaster, unless you don't mind making lots of mistakes ... it's about creating the capacity for surprise and learning in the context of one's work. That's why I'm suspicious of expertise; experts are people who are deeply involved in what they already know, and I don't want to be one of them.
>
> (Phillips et al. 2019, p. 240)

Tucker viewed the work contributing to her dismissal as a positive catalyst. She began work founding a new independent institution the very day she was fired:

> Right from the start the name 'New Museum' signalled an intentional paradox: this would not be a traditional institution, and it would not be bureaucratic, hierarchical, or centred around a permanent collection. However, it would maintain the seriousness and promote the scholarship of a museum. Tucker envisaged an alternative to conventional art institutions, a place where discovery and risk-taking were encouraged, where artists could experiment, where leading edge research would be conducted, where ever-new ideas about art were embraced, and where the character of the 'museum' could be redefined.
>
> (Phillips 2017, p. 8)

A significant feature of this, and all anti-museums, is securing financial independence from governmental sources. Over the years Tucker used her considerable social networks to secure donors, which came in the form of both cash and eventually, a significant building on Broadway. In this way, it was safely removed from the conservative forces of professional interest or political direction.

Alana Heiss admired Tucker's indefatigable activism. She told Battaglia (2017):

> She was a committed political figure of the '60s and early '70s variety. She believed she could make a difference, as a person and as a leader. She would get behind causes and pull the museum up to them.... She was particularly interested in feminist activity and feminist theory, which she bonded and represented in shows at the New Museum. She was the first on the block to show women doing this and women doing that. She was an icon to many disadvantaged or marginalized groups.... She wanted to copy the museum [concept] exactly but have it be a more important museum.

An evolving force

The New Museum opened in 1977, when very few museums were showing contemporary art in New York. In its prospectus, they claimed to be the only museum in New York to prioritise 'living artists and the work they make'. Its present Director, Lisa Philips, argued that 'this still holds true today. We've always been a future-facing museum – not a place for preserving and recording history, but a place where history is made' (Phillips 2017, p. 9).

For its first 30 years, the New Museum operated out of several relatively small spaces. In 1977, its first HQ was just an office in the Fine Arts Building on Hudson Street and it exhibited at a few locations off-site (Philips 2017, p. 353). Later, they were given gallery space at The New School for Social Research, at 65 5th Avenue. Tucker identified a significant role for the New Museum as an exhibitionary platform for contemporary artists marginalised, by race or gender, and emerging artists, unshown at commercial galleries, or ignored by the major New York museum tastemakers (Rifkin 2017, pp. 74–75).

To begin with her idea was to collect a work from everyone they exhibited, but this was discontinued. They did not wish to be distracted away from the immediacy and potency of contemporary art. At that time, exhibitions composed of unknown and unrecognised contemporary artists could easily be low key affairs in the wrong hands, but there was something fresh, new and upbeat about the way Tucker presented these artists. They weren't just new to the scene, they were a different, colourful and exciting and this impression was driven home by provocative, racy titles, enigmatic descriptions and unconventional venues in new public places. This started with their second show *New Work/New York* (1977) and they followed up with *Bad Painting* (1978), *In a Pictorial Framework* (1979), *The Art of Memory/The Loss of History* (1985) and *Bad Girls* (1994).

These were no ordinary titles valorised by worthy art historical references. Like the exhibitions they represented, satirical as well as slapstick humour was used to gain attention and also to make serious statements. Their punk shtick for a punk era caught on, and with access acquired to a ground floor display window ('The Window') on 14th Street, they introduced vibrant new contemporary art to a passing street public. It was a good stunt and it won them an audience they could never have persuaded through their door. 'The Window' series helped launch the early careers of Richard Prince, John Ahearn, Jeff Koons and David Hammons. In time, they moved to staging shows of the earlier work of newly established artists enjoying success in New York. Tucker's curation was controversial and combined with their 'insider' status, attracted a new generation of New York artists who gradually made New Museum their home.

In 1983, with wind in their sails, they received a significant donation of space in the Astor Building at 583 Broadway in SoHo. This was some 22,000 square feet on three floors, with an exhibition space in two shop windows, one on Broadway, and one on Mercer Street, at street level. In this way, they increased their passing public exposure on one of the world's busiest high streets, albeit a low status section of it. It was a perfect place for a young, clever, and confronting Adrian Piper to challenge white passers-by with her anti-racist performance provocations (Wallis 2017, p. 143).

In the 24 years they were at 583 Broadway, they staged the first major New York museum exhibitions of Andres Serrano, Adrian Piper, Christian Boltanski, Chris Ofili, Hans Haake, Nancy Spiro, David Wojnarowicz, Paul McCarthy, John Waters and many others. They had become a solid part of the New York scene, a significant nursery for what would become a world leading hotbed of contemporary art and had branched out beyond New York and the USA. It was on the global circuit, just about.

A new New Museum

Owing to its lean, small-scale operation and being an embedded insider of the SoHo art scene, it was limited in terms of its audience reach; it was off the tourist map and it could no longer fulfil the exhibitionary needs of the artists it had cultivated. When Whitney Museum curator Lisa Phillips succeeded Marcia Tucker in 2006, Phillips felt the New Museum was at a crossroads and should expand. They had to find and adapt yet another older building or build a new museum. Phillips built a new museum, according to their needs, where they needed to be.

The new New Museum took seven years of planning to build and was the first ground up, freestanding building on the Bowery and the first art museum built Downtown. This had the desired effect of lifting the New Museum onto a higher level, a proper international museum player yet with continuing commitments to its old locality. The move enabled them to increase their annual attendance from 60,000 to 400,000, quadruple their exhibition space, staff and budget and build a larger board, 'with veterans; and a steady infusion of young trustees with means' (Kennedy 2017). A year later they acquired the warehouse building on their south side to permit further expansion. In a very short time, they had expanded their activism too, and this required more than just gallery space. This was a smart move: while the property on Broadway had grown in value considerably, the land and buildings of ugly, unloved Bowery were still very cheap; yet it was still close to where so many artists lived and worked.

Activism

The New Museum is first and foremost an openly, politically driven institution, in the sense of remaining steadfastly true to the notion of art as inherently interested in how we live, how we think about changing the way we live and how we go about responding to externalities of all kinds. It is as much interested in the politics of museums as it is in the museum as a primary focus for political thinking, debate and dissemination of politically relevant ideas and socially engaged art (Sachs Olsen, 2019). As Brian Wallis (2017, p. 139) argued:

> The provocative notion that the museum could be more than an idealistic and politically disengaged space for leisure and aesthetic contemplation and could be an active forum for debate about public issues and everyday life was in many ways the defining ethos of the New Museum. Tucker was genuinely interested in testing the extent to which museums could become an evolving political statement, a social microcosm and an experimental laboratory where both art and the practices of the institution itself were always in question. To what extent could the museum articulate the social meanings of art and political activism?

According to Lucy R. Lippard, who wrote a 1984 catalogue for the New Museum exhibition *Art and Ideology*, activism also meant, 'a practice in which some element of the art takes place in the "outside world"' (Wallis 2017, p. 139). Wallis identified three notable areas where the New Museum has had enduring influence and impact: through the institutional critique of museums; through criticism and theory of public space; and through the role of collectives in socially engaged art.

There is a sense in which this form of activism was also the raison d'être of the New Museum as it experimented with, or attempted to operationalise, the aspirations and ideas of artists in the world outside the museum. It took on the role of cultural intermediary through its close relationship with artists, its immediate community of SoHo, and the Bowery and its wider global network of collaborators. Being an arts activist established its character as a different art institution and allowed that which was outlawed at the Whitney to blossom in the Bowery and elsewhere. As Phillips (2017, p. 24) observes:

> As we enter our fifth decade, the New Museum can claim both longevity and a continued relevance that could not have been anticipated in 1977. We remain open, fearless, and alive, and we keep evolving, asking the hard questions, challenging preconceptions and embracing the role that art and culture can play in this fast-changing landscape. Without the weight of collection, we are freer to experiment, explore, and respond to the new.

Under Tucker's and then Lisa Philip's leadership they have been especially active in the fields of women's art and in culture-led community development, city reconstruction and augmented public spheres.

Feminist and women's art

Against a New York art museum and gallery world that had singularly failed to produce gender equality among the artists shown (as demonstrated graphically by the Guerrilla Girls) (Ryzik 2015), the New Museum was a standout. Since opening, over 50 per cent of the artists exhibited were women (as compared with a 16 per cent average across 33 of New York's major galleries); all directors have been women and women have been prominent among their leadership (Phillips 2017, p. 14).

More broadly, they have supported feminist art, and art that interrogates gender, the body and sexuality very strongly, through the work of Adrian Piper, Martha Rosler, Mary Kelly and Rosemary Trockel in their earlier days, through to later shows by Sharon Hayes, Phyllida Barlow, Tacita Dean, Pipilotti Rist and Sarah Lucas (Smith 2017). As Lynne Tillman (2017), argues, many of their shows were overtly and distinctly themed in ways that emphasised feminism as dynamic and multi-focussed. They founded Artemis in 2015, a fund to support shows and projects by women.

Increasing the diversity of artists has always been linked to the development of diversity of audiences at the New Museum. For example, Deputy Director Karen Wong told me that Chris Ofili's show *Night and Day* in

2014/2015 made a palpable difference to the numbers of people of colour visiting the museum:

> I would say, the excitement around Chris Ofili's show was how it drew in the most people of colour I had seen at the museum, after being here for six or seven years. We were thinking, 'Oh, is this demographic going to come back again?' And I would say, since that show, we have continually built up a more inclusive audience.

Karen Wong also told me that they now have many students of colour visiting the museum after school, especially on Fridays. So, they may be laying down a new generation who will continue to normalise museum-going through their lives.

Community and city activism

Through their engagement with their locality and partner cities around the world the New Museum has championed interventions around urban redevelopment, gentrification, homelessness and poverty. In 2010, these themes were brought together in a new project called *Ideas City*, the brainchild of Deputy Director Karen Wong and Lisa Phillips. Extending an earlier project called *Museum as Hub*, which developed the idea of a museum having partners in collaboration to address common interests and becoming a platform for civic action, *Ideas City* responded to a paradox of their own creation. Grima (2017, p. 290) puts this well:

> Having chosen to relocate to one of the sites in New York most beloved by artists, it might, by virtue of its very presence, contribute to making the neighbourhood inaccessible to those it was there to serve: other non-profits, organisations and entire communities that had made Lower Manhattan an epicentre of creativity and leadership in the arts.

The gravity of this situation was also compounded by the clustering of galleries into 'art gallery districts', first in Soho and then Chelsea (around the newly constructed High Line that culminates at the new Whitney), as the growing literature on art-led gentrification specific to this area attests (Matthews 2010; Ganning 2016; Sasajima 2016; Schuetz 2014). Building on New York's tradition of street festivals, the New Museum used this popular cultural form to gather together a collective response on a full weekend in May 2011. Their shared purpose was to keep the idea of a local tradition of art alive, to increase their mutual visibility locally and internationally, and to respond to the notion that design and architecture alone does not make liveable cities. As Judd observed back in the 1970s, design and architecture is more often on the side of development and rising rents than maintaining good art or artists in place. Through the New Museum, this festive collective was also able to involve the Mayor of New York, which opened lines of communication between politicians and the arts community (Grima 2017, pp. 290–291). Karen Wong told me that this festival aimed to show that a number of local organisations could collaborate as partners, amplify each other's voices and provide a platform for all the younger, smaller and ground-up organisations in Downtown to present their ideas. The local organisations came to the festival like vendors in a street market, except they were required to sell an idea for the city. There were also conferences and panels where, as Karen Wong explained, 'it was a moment for us to, say "we should be at the table when everybody starts reimagining the city"'.

Gradually, *Ideas City* evolved sub-initiatives such as its five-day residency program where 40 Fellows were chosen (one-third from the city, one-third from the host country and one-third from international locations), the idea being 'to produce critical and creative responses to the conditions they encounter on the ground' (Grima 2017, p. 293). Its success spawned others held in Detroit and Athens in 2016, and in Arles, France in 2017 and subsequently in Istanbul and San Palo. *Ideas City* proposed new ways of making the work of an arts-based institution relevant to the reality of a rapidly urbanising world, it changed the perception of art and culture as superfluous luxuries and linked the spheres of design, policy and administration to the 'critical practice of art as essential to civic life' (Grima 2017, p. 293). The New Museum continued to shine a path along a route where museum and artist travel together and to preserve their historic spatial settings in places of their own making.

Humour and activism

The centrality and seriousness of their activism should not leave the impression that the New Museum ever lost their defining and edgy sense of humour. As in the early days, humour in the form of satire, parody, irreverence and mockery, is a critical element of the activist art they like to exhibit. Humour is valuable because it provokes a reaction, hailing something already within an audience that establishes a connection to the art, while at the same time, aligning the audience to its direction and force. It's simple and direct: if you laugh along with it, you get it.

Humour is a powerful tool for activism because it sustains a critical point of view and a political intervention, without proselytising, cajoling or high-mindedness. It was in humour that traditional carnival found a political voice and formed social solidarity around it, and this voice has been reactivated in much of the contemporary art that the New Museum likes to show (Connelly 2003; Cross 2006). Whereas many conventional museums avoid aligning themselves with the fierceness and direction of contemporary art, anti-museums embrace it and enhance it. There is a something of a wilting disconnect for audiences when conventional museums show obviously political works of contemporary art but make only weak art historical points by way of highlighting its 'importance' or value 'as art'. Such representations rob the art of its capacity to reach out to its audience, in its own terms.

No such art historical mediation or gloss attended Nathaniel Mellors' *Progressive Rocks*, a series of videos, attendant props, animatronic installations, and paintings that I saw on my museum tour of the New Museum in April 2018. In true anti-museum theatre style, *Progressive Rocks* is encountered in a gloaming light, with its colourful paintings and grotesque props picked out by bright spotlights. A lot of art world mythologies and problems are tackled satirically by staging them in future or past scenarios that allow their absurdity to be given full expression. In his review the critic William Corwyn found

> cheeky, hairy, and streetwise homo neanderthalensis geezers who have smug and nihilistic answers to questions about their species' art-making and cultural capabilities.... [They] discuss or engage in making art, and then attempt to, or actually do manage to eat their homo sapiens companions
>
> (Corwyn 2018)

Essentially, it's the same gag as the Monty Python's Art Gallery sketch (see p. 16), but all the better for daring to be truly nasty and global; hitting home on wider structures of power and attitudes to diversity.

Mellors' show was a tour de force of absurdist, satirical parody of art and human pretension, tackling national mythologies, religion and authority structures. While it is technically well executed, its low key, low budget sparing minimalism focuses our attention on its gloriously rich and sharp language. It is easily strong enough to sustain an audience through its 300 minutes of run time and was right on message for the New Museum, who presented it masterfully in their newly inaugurated South Galleries, a space designated for premiering new productions.

Sarah Lucas: Au Naturel, her first major US retrospective, was on at the New Museum when I visited again, in December 2018. It was a relief to hit Broadway and leave behind uptown shops full of tawdry Christmas

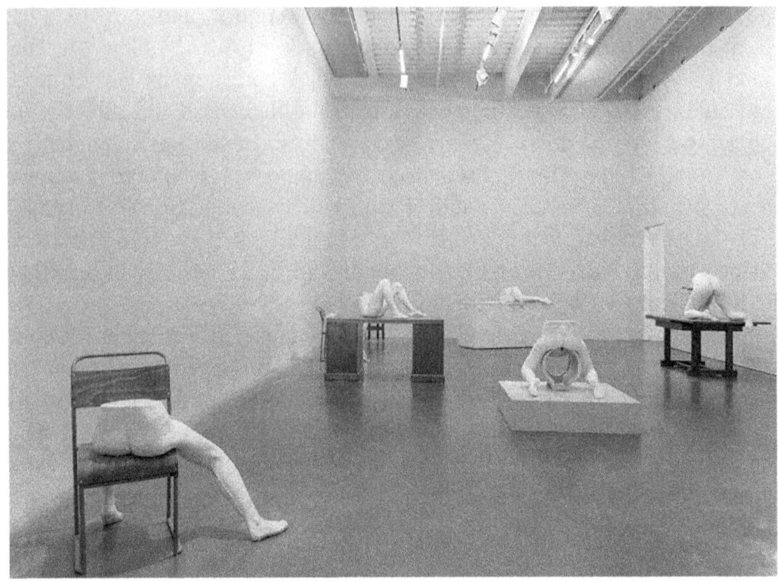

Figure 4.4 Installation view: 'Sarah Lucas: Au Naturel', New Museum, New York, 2018. Courtesy the artist and New Museum

Photo: EPW Studio

luxuries to finally see her 'two fried eggs and a kebab' on an old table. I've been laughing at this for 20 years. This was a star of one of my favourite shows *Sensation*, and of one of my favourite art books, *Sarah Lucas* by Matthew Collings (2003). Sarah Lucas, the thinking gallery-goer's sculptor, who uses her own body and discarded things around her to object to and modify the arbitrary and strange conventions of femininity, sexuality and gender. Her response was to explore what it feels like as a woman to refuse them (and thus be released from them) and then to gaze again at its odd material expression in everyday life. It was her own unique angle revealed through humour and wit. Why were cigarettes and smoking associated more strongly with dominant masculinity? Why was it 'funny' when a cigarette was left poked into the anus or a vulva of her sculptures of female anatomy? Why is 'two eggs and a kebab', such an offensive remark in English men's pub talk, and yet also funny when rendered into art. Why was she so interested in 'the penis'? Rather than rejecting the puerile, the lavatorial, the pornographic or disgusting, these became her new starting points for an enquiry into human embodiment, referenced in popular culture by its rich material iconography of the everyday.

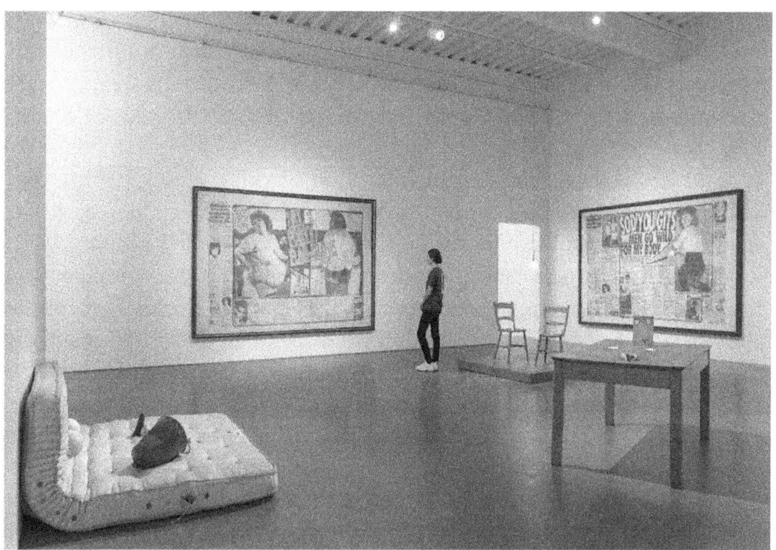

Figure 4.5 Installation view: 'Sarah Lucas: Au Naturel', New Museum, New York, 2018. Courtesy the artist and New Museum

Photo: EPW Studio

In the brilliant catalogue of the Lucas show, Maggie Nelson's essay tells us how important it had been for her to 'get' Lucas back in the 1990s. Nelson (2018, p. 12) appreciated how the New Museum had avoided locating, or reducing, Lucas to the art historical narrative of a former associate of a once-infamous art group; where she might have been presented as 'the mellowing of an angry feral soul'. Lucas had been a key part of 'an international network of punk, DIY, woman-artist-run spaces fuelled by experiment, brazenness, pleasure and humour – the like of which we needed back then [1980s] and frankly could use more of now' (Nelson 2018, p. 12). Yes, but until they all arrive, the current Lucas will still carry the day.

Conclusion

New Museum clearly meets the general criteria of an anti-museum in that they programmatically reversed core characteristics of conventional museums. Mara Gladstone (2012, pp. 192–193) argues that the archives of the New Museum during the 1970s and 1980s, many of them personal exchanges between artists and Marcia Tucker, 'offer a deep view into the history of one of the forebears of the anti-museum movement, of which P.S.1 (opened in 1976) and the Pompidou Centre in Paris (opened in 1977) were also brethren'. Tucker's pioneering commitment to living contemporary art, which she evolved through her New Museum experiment, is seen as a 'prescient and viable centrepiece for more than three decades' (Gladstone 2012, p. 192).

In these 30 years, the emphasis was on working closely with artists, facilitating their art, and supporting their art practice as much as it was merely curating and exhibiting their art. Tucker avoided aspirations for collections, art history and didacticism and concentrated on supporting artists whose works in performance, installations and digital forms tested the limits of the traditional media. Beyond founding an anti-museum, she was also a significant player in the expansion of conceptual art in New York and America. In this work and aspiration, Tucker followed in the footsteps of Judd's broader aim for museums to build a structure for art and artists rather than architecture.

The New Museum is similar to the Collection de l'Art Brut in that both chose to exhibit art that is disruptive of conventional art museums: art brut because it questions the creativity, exclusivity and legitimacy of academic art and activist contemporary art because it renders art history an irrelevant distraction from the true destiny of art, which is to make history. Not art about art but art about life. It is easy to take the growth and popularity of contemporary art for granted in recent times, certainly since 2000, but it might not have happened were it not for anti-museums like PS1 and the New Museum. They showed that transformative and political art could find institutional support, though as Terry Smith (2012) has shown, these institutions also became models for a new breed of collectors of contemporary art.

Collectors also began to establish significant and well-resourced new private museums all around the world, and following pioneers like PS1 and the New Museum, they too developed special relationships with artists. The more that the growing number of private collector enthusiasts bid up the cost of contemporary art, the more conventional museums fell behind in their capacity to build representative collections. And, the more the new collectors built exhibitionary spaces especially for specific works (after the style of Judd, Heiss and Tucker), the less appealing the conventional museum gallery became to contemporary artists anyway. The older public art museums could not hang all or even most of their collection and to have new works make only brief appearances also held little appeal for contemporary artists, whose works addresses the present. Gradually there was what Gnyp (2015) called 'the shift'; away from conventional art museums towards private collectors' and other private museums and not-for-profits. And, as we will now see in the next case, of The Museum of Old and New Art (Mona) in Hobart, Australia, the anti-museum concept had certainly not run its course. It would continue to oppose convention in ever new and startling ways, from remote and unexpected places, and through charismatic individuals with resources and determination.

5 Mona (Museum of Old and New Art), Hobart

Introduction

The Museum of Old and New Art (Mona) opened on 22 January 2011 in Hobart, on the island state of Tasmania, off the southeastern coast of Australia. For many it is a very remote place, some 8,766 km from Tokyo, 16,619 km from New York, and 17,391 km from London. It is handy for Antarctica though, a mere 2,640 km away.

Mona is built in the working-class suburb of Berriedale, in the City of Glenorchy (part of Greater Hobart), which is in the top decile of social disadvantage in Australia. Yet it is set in the Arcadian vineyard of Moorilla Estate that occupies a striking promontory of the River Derwent, and looks across to the prospect of magnificent wooded plains and a world class mountain wilderness in the distance. Fish eagles, dolphins and seals hunt the waters around it. Within sight of Mona lies the wreck, visible at low tide, of the sailing barque *Otago*, a ship once captained by Joseph Conrad, the author of *Heart of Darkness*. Once a sacred place of Aboriginal gathering, this interstitial, auspicious location is now a star in the art world firmament.

When Mona opened, it caught the eye of the art world press immediately: every major arts magazine, journal and newspaper despatched reporters south who filed a series of breathless accolades (Franklin 2014). It was also praised by major museum directors, art critics and academics. In a museum sector jaded by serial repetition and star architect design escalation, with mostly conventional white cube galleries on the inside, here was something else; something unimagined before, a completely different kind of art museum altogether. Its owner, David Walsh, a mathematical maven who had beaten the gambling industry at its own game, called it variously an anti-museum, and a subversive adult Disneyland. Initially its twin themes were sex and death. Walsh told Richard Flanagan that he aimed to piss off academic museum and art world types

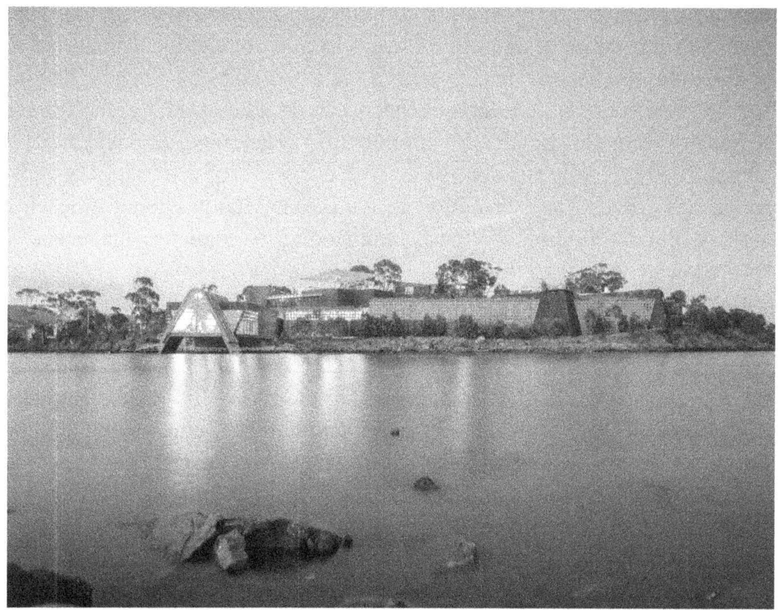

Figure 5.1 Mona

Photo credit: Mona/Jesse Hunniford. Image courtesy of Mona, Museum of Old and New Art, Hobart, Tasmania, Australia

(Flanagan 2013). He did irritate a few, but to *his* annoyance the vast majority fell in love with Mona, despite themselves. In this chapter, it will be revealed how Mona's key innovation was in visitor engagement and designing a place where encountering art would become deeply pleasurable as well as challenging and possibly life changing in some way. It became a very attractive place for artists as well as musicians, to work and exhibit, and so began the second life of a major collector of contemporary art: working closely with artists after the manner of Judd, PS1, and the New Museum.

A subversive adult Disneyland?

Building and funding Mona to the tune of approximately $100 million, Walsh looked on perplexed and disappointed as the accolades rolled in. He had hoped that his thorough and irreverent reversal of the conventional art museum would draw fire, controversy and scandal, and, in a way, that was a reasonable expectation. Conventional museums are conservative, and they stay close to international norms (Green 2018). Some people did not like it at all, but mostly Mona's style of anti-museum worked too well: reversing the aims, design and delivery of the conventional museum so completely, so cheekily, and on such a scale proved to be a heady, liberating experience – as if everyone had secretly been waiting for this to happen (Timms 2011a, 2011b; Croome 2011; Hanquinet & Savage 2012; Capon 2013). That it was done by an irreverent, clever working-class Australian only boosted its reception in Australia. Mona was not quiet, not serious, not sombre, not hectoring, not finding its audience inadequately formed or in need of instruction.

Walsh told Sharon Verghis of *The Australian* that Mona 'continues out from how I see the world, it rarefied how I see the world ... that's why I built the gallery – to essentially be an anti-museum and to look at art a little bit differently' (Verghis 2016). That was an understatement. Such were the art world rumours in the year before Mona opened that the (New York- and London-based) *Art Newpaper* despatched Christina Ruiz to check it out. Ruiz had seen everything but Mona took her breath away:

> Imagine a museum which overturns virtually every accepted notion of institutional practice: an underground museum with no natural light, with a deliberately confusing design so visitors get lost as they wander through its halls, and a museum which, in places, is incredibly noisy and very, very smelly.... He is keen to stress there will be no formal curatorship. 'I believe most curation is bullshit ... curators tie together a bunch of stuff they can get their hands on then create the most abstruse and obtuse reality and, in the end, fill an exhibition up with a few things that are slightly connected and the upshot is that about 30% of the art is just there to fill space.'
>
> (Christina Ruiz *Art Newspaper* (2010))

David Walsh was not in awe of the art world, much of which he thought silly, self-serving and pompous. He was not always impressed by the art or the artists either, even some of the ones he had acquired. He did not take his inspiration from a deep reading of the anti-museum literature either. As he told me:

> I was thinking about museums as temples, as being a place to worship at a particular facility that the state exposes you to. And I wanted to democratise that. I didn't realise when I used that term that others had used it in a similar, but not identical context.
>
> (David Walsh, interview with author, 19 May 2018)

If he believed in anything it was, like Marcia Tucker, in the as-yet-unrealised potential of museums. He had been a great fan of museums all his life but had become disappointed by them ultimately. He felt a strong urge to do something about it.

While Mona's design and display were going to be radically new, these were not ends in themselves. He was mostly attempting to alter the experience people have with art in quite practical ways. In a 2011 interview, he told Peter Hill that:

> I want no labelling or visual explanation on the wall. I don't want to create expectations or pre-judge your responses. The need to explain works with interpretive material vanished with the internet. *I want to create a need to know.* If people leave more curious than when they arrive then that would be a good outcome.
>
> (Hill 2011, p. 46, my emphasis)

Here he shares some considerable kinship with Judd, Heiss and Tucker.

Walsh and his team planted doubts about the authority of museums, mocked the pretentions of the art world and had no interest in sowing rival narratives. As he told me, 'The Mona path can't be like the circumambulation of the Kaaba, or the Stations of the Cross; there can't be enlightenment at the end' (DW, interview with Adrian Franklin, January 2019). But he saw the symbolism and the language of authority as inscribed in the architecture and communications of the modern conventional museum as a major problem, a barrier to engagement by those who had yet to develop dispositions toward art. The very people they were meant to be reaching.

Walsh appeared to know instinctively that authority always presented itself in a serious way and was vulnerable to mockery and laughter. These were the guardians of unthought, or received ideas that Rabelais called *agélastes*, those who do not laugh, the enemies of art (Kundera 2006). Walsh was quite prepared to do the unthinkable and begin to mock the overconfident and proud fraternity of the art museum. He was as dismissive and vocal as Judd had been, but instead of turning his back on the museum, he intended to show, like Tucker before him, how something *like a museum* might yet succeed if it was transformed sufficiently from within. In another interview in 2010 Walsh made what he was doing clear. He told John Bastable (2010, p. 100) that '[Mona] is going to be a subversive adult Disneyland. My intent is serious but the process is comic'. And Walsh was quite prepared to play the clown (Franklin 2014).

By 2017, it was clear that Mona was not just a scaled-up biennale stunt or a flash-in-the pan commercial venture. It had serious intent, it followed through its on its promises and aims and it maintained the momentum. In Rose Lang's SBS broadcast (2017), 'A tour through the best museums in Australia' she said:

> MONA is inspiring as a museum with an anarchic, melodramatic and unapologetically partisan approach to contemporary art. Its liberating rock n' roll take on everything it does has made audiences and the gatekeepers of contemporary art question their assumptions about the fundamentals of making a museum and a few key things about looking at art. The anti-museum museum.

Aside from the showbiz styling, Mona's serious intent was also beginning to be valued by museological scholars. According to Janice Baker (2012):

> At a number of levels, [Mona] raises interesting critical questions. It seeks to avoid visitors feeling anxious because they are supposed to conform to cultural codes of viewing including knowing a whole lot about art. Reducing such anxiety is a central concern today for the public museum where commitment to 'accessibility' and 'inclusion' is an expectation. However, while wanting to create an accessible space, MONA simultaneously seeks to avoid the stasis of conformity that accompanies the earnestness that comes with the 'audience-focussed' museum. The degree to which MONA provides the opportunity for a new type of attention to art through managing this tension; of not being beholden to 'museum correctness' while forging a space of its own that is nevertheless accessible, is a challenge of critical interest.
>
> (Baker, 2012 (podcast))

Even the most senior art museum Directors in Australia conceded that something remarkable had happened inside Mona: Edmund Capon (2013), former Director of The Art Gallery of New South Wales argued that: 'In Australia maybe the future has already arrived at a place that redefines the term art gallery … forced us to see art in a different way'.

Visiting Mona

Approached from the water on one of its art and alcohol-filled fast ferries, Mona looks like a coastal citadel, built heavy to defend a vulnerable port city or desert oasis. Across the narrow shoreline a pier connects the boat landing to a set of steep stairs cut into thick Jurassic sandstone cliffs. Visitors are obliged to climb these, and much thought went into their role for engaging with the museum. Much experimentation and effort went into making sure that these steps can be walked at a slow, processional speed, one step at a time, by way of reminding visitors that they are entering a ritual space, where they must prepare themselves to be changed in some way. Technically, such steps breached building regulations but their worthy purpose and beauty swayed the inspector.

At the top, visitors are confounded by a large open plaza, with views out across a narrow bay to a small island with Mount Wellington forming a spectacular backdrop. Dominating the plaza, somewhat bizarrely, is a functional tennis court with other stairs and paths leading away to other buildings. It is not clear where you are at this point and there are no signs to help. There is an alarmingly, disconcerting distorting mirror on the right-hand side of the tennis court, and a trampoline to the left. ‘Could we have gone the wrong way?’ ‘Isn’t this a private residence?’, we think. As our eyes study the scene more closely, a small door can be seen in the middle of the mirror. This is the entrance; no, the *aperture* into Mona. We are being toyed-with on some kind of Alice in Wonderland trip. We are reduced to a childish impulse to enter the funfair. We go in.

Or not. Some find it so bizarrely opposed to what would be a creditable museum entrance that they miss the portal and carry on looking for a

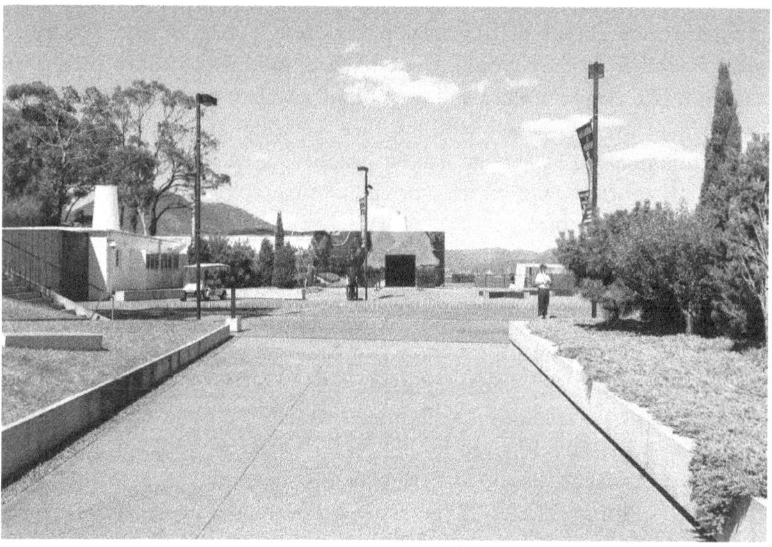

Figure 5.2 Mona entrance and plaza during *Gilbert & George: The Art Exhibition*

Photo credit: Mona/Rémi Chauvin. Image courtesy Mona, Museum of Old and New Art, Hobart, Tasmania, Australia

proper museum entrance. Had we veered away from this obscure portal, as some do, we would have found ourselves suddenly in something even less convincing: a pastoral scene, at the top of a beautiful vineyard that slopes down for a long way, with views across to Mount Wellington. Here there are several large new buildings standing around a level green, with a large sound stage built at the far end, yet it has a rustic, mellow feel. There is a wine bar, a winery, a cellar door and a brewery too. Occasionally, a hen and her chicks break cover from the vines or the olive grove and trail across the green, pecking calmly. On other occasions, a flock of guinea fowl might be seen between rows of pinot noir. Wild rabbits nibble grass here and there; there's something like Museo Delores Olmedo's homely feel here. There are smart and expensive-looking architectural accommodation pods nestling into the cliff top on the other side of the green. At times, guests break cover from these. It is not clear where to go from here. It is not clear what kind of place we are in.

The scene, then, is a disorientating rustic-surreal, yet it also reminded me of the location used for the cult British TV show *The Prisoner*, mostly all shot at the weird and otherworldly resort at Portmeirion, Wales. Or the home of a Bond villain. To have almost no signs creates an eerie feeling for such a large place as Moorilla; but then again, it doesn't have a gatehouse, a security barrier or a ticket office at the front entrance to the estate either. It is part of the radical informality (another reversal of convention) insisted on by David Walsh, and, in fact, people wander onto the estate grounds rather as they would a public park, take walks, have picnics or drop into the wine bar café and they often stay late on summer evenings. David Walsh was born to a working class Catholic family on a neighbouring public housing estate and used to wander past this estate when it was closed off to locals and entirely private. I suspect that, too, factored into his reverse design thinking.

Obviously, visitors from afar are lost without directions, and such is their absence that the dark thought soon occurs to them that this is entirely deliberate. Eighty-eight per cent of visitors to Mona (350,000+ per year) have flown into Hobart. Every now and again other lost souls arrive from the opposite direction, either walking into view across the lawn, or appearing abruptly on a small lane winding its way through the vineyard. They have driven by car or arrived by bus and they too are looking in vain for directions. As far as we know everyone finds the entrance, eventually. That they must do this through their own volition, make decisions on where they go and what to do/see is central to one of the ways Walsh has reversed the status/performance of visitors to art museums. Away from those assumed to be in need of instruction, direction and improvement to those who, as respected, culturally formed individuals, can be trusted and encouraged to self-direct themselves to an engagement of their own choosing. And from there to develop a deeper interest, or not. Treat people as adults, even children, and they will rise to the task of engaging with art. It is perfectly OK not to like it. The giving of responsibility and trust to visitors is there at the outset, and applied consistently afterwards. There are no guided tours. You are very much on your own.

Once through the narrow aperture, visitors are greeted by friendly staff and quickly processed into the lobby, off which there is a cloakroom, a bookshop and a café and beyond that a lawn with chairs and more stunning views. The building is elegant but stripped-back, and there is a seating area close to a spectacular modern fireplace and chimney with huge windows looking over the estate towards the mountain. It is really homely rather than institutionally or aesthetically aloof; this, too, was deliberate. And also, because it *is* the original home of the Alcorsos, in a relatively plain Spanish style. Mona itself is built deep beneath it and stretches unseen, underground to join up with the other Roy Grounds building, The Round House, some considerable distance away. In fact, by a miraculous feat of engineering, the Alcorso house now floats above Mona, suspended between its heavy subterranean concrete pillars. Visitors can look up from a glorious bar two floors underground and marvel at the exposed footings of the original building. So, here's another new thing for most visitors. You arrive at a prestigious museum and yet it is nowhere to be seen. Instead, there are two 1950s building minding their own business in a rurally idyllic vineyard setting.

At the centre of the lobby is a narrow staircase that spirals around the shaft for a space-age cylindrical lift, in Archigram style. Both the stairs and the lift go down 14 metres (46 feet) into the ground, through layers of solid Jurassic sandstone rock, and through two floors of subterranean gallery spaces. It is uncanny going down this far, or spiralling down endless steps. Down is somehow dangerous.

Lost in art

Visitors are not given a map, there are no directions or routes indicated and there are no signs or labels inside Mona. Visitors are on their own. They must make all the decisions on where to go, what to see and for how long. Perhaps they would like a drink? There is a seductively amicable cocktail bar waiting for them as they arrive at the deepest level. It is dark. Any time seems right for a drink down there.

The museum has not been divided into obvious themes or sections; there is no chronology or taxonomy, so there is no need for signs to specific places. In fact, the museum interior, which is labyrinthine and

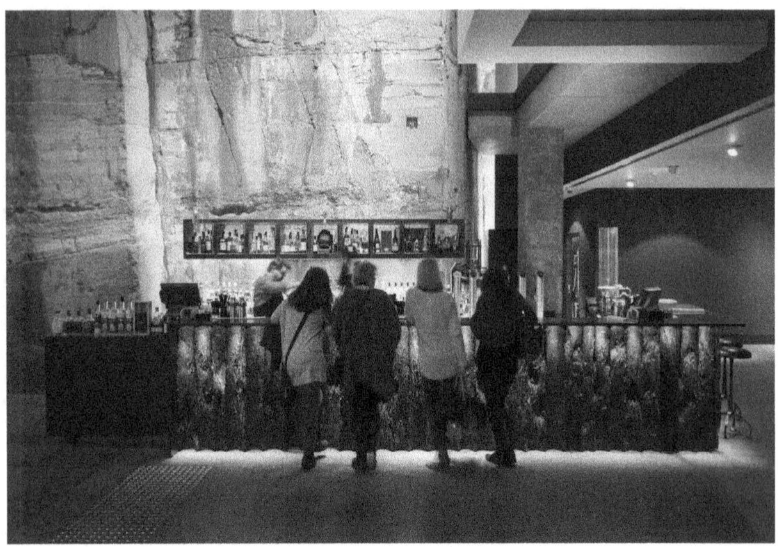

Figure 5.3 Void Bar

Photo credit: Mona/Rémi Chauvin. Image courtesy Mona, Museum of Old and New Art, Hobart, Tasmania, Australia

mysterious, throws up options and crossroads rather than directions. It is fairground now, with an unusual touch of class. The building is essentially low-cost brutalism, not far from the style of a concrete multi-story car park, but it's so dark you don't notice. In fact, it looks dramatic when seen with art lit in pools of light. What you do notice are the amazing hand-crafted appointments everywhere: the blacksmith-made door handles, the old red leather cinema seats sourced from Milan, the arts and crafts detailing for the bar. Such great care was taken with everything, that it merges seamlessly with the spectacular art itself. The art is installed in a beautiful way that gives the visitor multiple options after viewing any one work, so that instead of sensing a museum tour in terms of following clear lines, there is a much stronger experience of following one's own nose. Amusing oneself. This is following in the picturesque style of gardens.

The art is installed in such a way that visitors must choose between several possible next moves, and as they zig-zag in chaotic lines of preference, so they forget all sense of direction, and where they are within the museum as a whole. Or any sense of where they *ought* to be.

It was an explicit design aim that visitors should become lost sooner than found. There are no central stairwells that take you out of one gallery and orient you in terms of floor or gallery – or how much further there is to go. Instead, there are specially made, meandering corten steel staircases which span the huge aerial spaces of the museum, lifting guests high above the floor they leave with oversight of several floors, above, beyond and below. There are a large number of possible routes in every direction, up and down, and all the while showing options, enticing the viewer. The picturesque style in landscape gardening was a conscious manipulation of elements so as to create scenes inside a picture, of foregrounds, middlegrounds, and backgrounds, multiple places for the eye to find wonderment. Here there are similarities with the anti-museum designed by artists Johannes Cladders (1968) and architect Hans Hollein at the Museum Abteiberg (1982) in Germany, notably 'the versatility of the prospects', 'the decentralisation of the rooms', 'the assymetrical structure and an anti-monumental approach' (Benedetti 2019).

Repetitiveness in the form of taxonomy which can break concentration and produce museum fatigue is avoided at Mona. Instead, Mona choreographs individually arresting works that sit quietly or noisily and alone in their own light, in the dark recesses of its galleries and catacombs. Here, there is considerable kinship with the Collection de l'Art Brut in Lausanne. Rather than following linear narratives of art history, Mona curates connections of juxtaposition that allow the art works from different times, cultures and places to resonate with each other.

In this way, Mona museum tours are different, consisting of loops and twists, often chancing upon works of interest several times or missing swathes of the collection only to be told about them, or find them later, or even after leaving – producing a wish to return. The works are encountered more like a carnival procession, works that crave attention, with noise, scale, shock, emotion and a pulsating resonance with contemporary life (Franklin 2014). A smart device (The 'O') is given free to everyone and can tell visitors what they are looking at, and can, if requested, deliver several forms of information, in different voices, about it. Their entire tour is sent to visitors electronically on leaving the museum so that their uniquely complex route through the museum is souvenired forever.

Walsh tends to collect works that are relevant to contemporary life, those that address in interesting ways pressing issues, political and cultural tensions, from the everyday to the epochal to the climatic (Franklin 2014). These include gender, sexuality, health, death, environment, technology, power, authority and violence. A lot of the works at Mona show how these issues are felt through the human body and as such, more or less anyone can relate to them since the artworks actively and quite deliberately *hail*

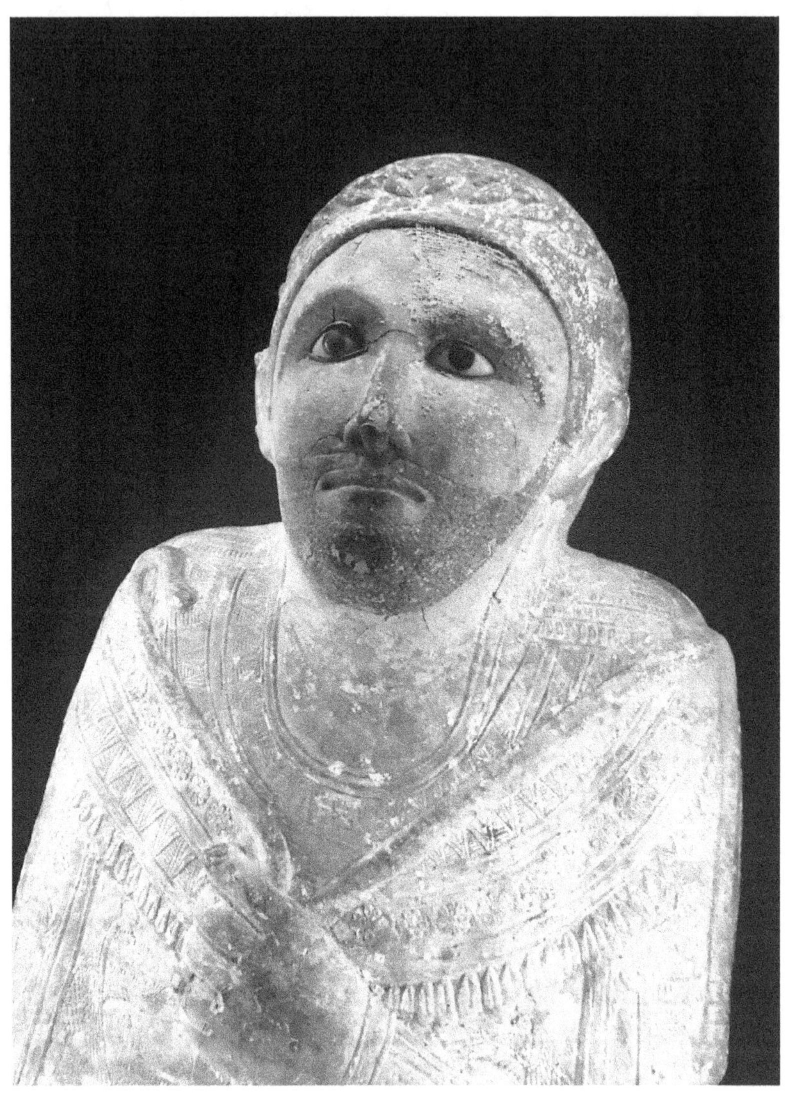

Figure 5.4 Death from another age: the coffin of Pausirus: Egypt 100 BCE–CE 100

Photo credit: Adrian Franklin. Image courtesy Mona, Museum of Old and New Art, Hobart, Tasmania, Australia

contemporary audiences. Mona is brave, unflinching and uncompromising in the art it shows and does not hesitate to include works that have been censored or excluded by other art institutions (e.g. Offili's Black Virgin Mary from the *Sensations* show in New York, cf. Chapter 3, p. 71), or cannot even be named by mainstream media (e.g. the ABC (Australia) Radio National censoring of Gregg Taylor and friends' (2008–2009) *Cunts ... and Other Conversations*). He has hung the much controversial and much vilified photographer, Bill Henson (Marr 2008). In 2018, Mona also hosted a major exhibition from the collection of James Brett's Museum of Everything, which included a strong list of works by art brut and other outsider artists.

Motives to build Mona

Mona is possibly one of the most thoroughly thought out, executed and funded anti-museums to date. It arose not merely from David Walsh's thoughts on the problems of the modern museum, it came from his previous experience of building a small museum of antiquities, taking a close interest in its design, running and impact and watching it fall short of its potential for visitors.

Walsh bought the Moorilla estate in 1995 at a time when he had embarked on an enthusiastic period of collecting antiquities. The vineyard business needed improving and to that end it needed a new function centre that would be elegant and new enough to scoop a large share of the function market in Tasmania. At the same time, he had run out of space for his collection and was looking for a means of storing or showing it. In the end, he combined the two so that functions would, effectively, be held in a museum of antiquities that could be open at all other times to vineyard visitors (Franklin 2014). He told me that without even thinking about it his museum soon turned into a conventional white cube. Partly this was because he hired professional curators and partly because he knew of no other model to follow. He worked especially hard to write accurate labels and was astounded by how hungry they were for space, how they vied for attention with the objects themselves and how all too easily visitors toured the labels rather than the objects.

Walsh loved ancient Greek coins and had collected some of the best in the world, yet whatever their rarity or beauty, visitors never 'gave them their due', as he and other collectors did (Benjamin 1955). He wondered why this was. He watched their restless manner among his collection. It rankled. He knew how much attention and thought he gave them, and how visitors to his home behaved differently with them, as they became topics of conversation. He also noticed how the function crowds looked at them, and how much more attention they gave them. The function crowds were attending the real rituals of their lives: betrothals, weddings, anniversaries, awards nights, parties – all of them important *transformational* rituals. People arriving at these were met with wines from the vineyard and were more socially effervescent and less socially inhibited, with the result that they viewed the same objects, many of which were also ritual objects, in a different way. They engaged the objects in noisy and animated discussions, involving laughter, joking, comments, comparisons with their own lives. How the same collection was able to switch between passive and active forms of engagement made an impression on Walsh. The labels were deemed a problem and they would not reappear when Mona was built.

As he shifted to collecting contemporary art on a global stage he quickly ran out of storage and his mind turned to building a much bigger museum. He began to acquire like-minded staff to help him first, build his collection, and then to help him identify new aims and character for a bigger, improved kind of museum. The design of the new museum was very important but changing visitor experience of art was of paramount importance.

Mona's museum brief

Walsh avoided hiring conventional art museum curators for Mona, and these, together with a range of other people, including architects, an engineer, a creative director, a museum designer, a librarian, the former manager of the antiquities museum, spent six years discussing and shaping what Mona would aim to be and do.

For a museum departing from, and critical of museological convention in art museums, they were heading into unknown territory, for which there were few existing models – although they did seek them out. They were variously impressed by Museo Delores Olmedo in Mexico City; The Soane Museum and the Wallace Collection, London; The Frick collection in New York and Le Palais Tokyo, Paris, but none of these were a model for what they were attempting to do at Moorilla.

Although the ideas that circulated in their discussions were slowly forming some substance, the design was most guided by what they wanted to avoid rather than knowing what they wanted to do instead. They therefore began to formulate a museum brief consisting of hero and value statements that their exhibition designer would eventually render into a three-dimensional form and visitor experience. Mona's museum Director, Mark Fraser, wrote a final version on 15 September 2007. It included the following points:

- Establish a museum culture at the forefront of the Australian art scene, with relevance on an international level. It will challenge conventional expectations as to what a museum is and how it interacts with the public.
- Our tone is loud, aggressive, relentless, subversive. It is a contradiction to the peaceful location.
- Challenge the visitors' pre-conceived notions of art through the juxtaposition of seemingly contradictory elements.
- Generate surprise and discovery by arousing curiosity and rewarding exploration – not just about individual items but about larger questions.
- Create an experience for visitors – David does not object to a 'fairground' experience. Strong emotions are welcome.
- Demonstrate that dumbing-down is unnecessary and that a community will rise to the level required for appropriate engagement with an entity.
- We need to be declarative of our ideas. We do not pretend to be objective (as most museums endeavour to be).
- Interpretive material should present dichotomies. We are prepared to attack ourselves. [Here Mona was removing itself as a voice of authority and an arbiter of taste].
- Disconcert non-free-thinkers with relentless assault of ideas.
- Challenge and confront visitors with topics currently regarded as taboo. Present exhibits that induce rage, polemics, emotively charged discourse.
- MONA's overarching messages are more significant than the individual objects in the collection.
- Old art is also contemporary – Roger M. Buergel (curator and theorist).

(Fraser 2013)

Taken together, these elements establish Mona's belonging to the family of anti-museums and they show just how diverse, if not unique, these are always likely to be. Aside from the numerous references to style, aesthetics, politics, pedagogy, technology and design we can distil three broad ways in which Mona's anti-museum intervention impacted exhibition and visitor engagement.

- Change the nature of engagement with the museum: to encourage an actively self-engaged encounter with the museum and its art by arousing states of wonderment and thought;
- Provide new ways of accessing art: to invite visitors to determine their pathways into art experiences – to determine their own response and to discover their own voice;

- Transform visitors' lives and consciousness: to provide a transformative experience – to change visitor's lives, in some way.

Leigh Carmichael, Mona's artistic director, condensed the museum brief even further into a brand description. He realised that while most conventional museums have only a very weak sense of brand (because they do not wish to differentiate themselves from convention), a strong sense of brand is important for those museums, i.e. anti-museums, that *really* do wish to depart from the norm. Thus, for Carmichael:

> Mona's brand values are: reason, radicalism, egalitarianism, pedagogy and pleasure.
> We will be: iconoclastic, radical, controversial, fun, brave.
> We will not be: conventional, didactic, highbrow, dumb, serious, dictated to.
>
> (Leigh Carmichael, cited in Franklin 2014, p. 168)

Mona's brand values were realised visually, and especially online, by Carmichael working alongside Elizabeth Pearce, Mona's writer. They established an arresting mix of gothic darkness with disquieting 'Twin Peaks' overtones, combined with irreverent, dark and self-deprecating humour, wrapped in a livery of 'sex shop pink'.

This branding resonates strongly with their collection. Many of the artworks are large and full of life and humour. Among the most popular works are Wim Delvoye's *Cloaca* (2010), an imposingly large, fiendishly scientific lab machine that mimics exactly the biochemistry of the human digestive system, such that it is fed in the morning and does a shit in late afternoon (no prizes for guessing which event is the more popular with Mona audiences). Julius Popp's mesmerising *bit.fall (2006–7)* forms the currently most frequently used words on Google from water droplets falling from ceiling height. These pulse out a rhythm that acts like a mechanical heart beat for the museum. *Cunts and Other Conversations* (2008–2009), by Gregg Taylor and friends, are 151 individually sculpted wall-mounted porcelain human vulvas modelled from women around the world, and representing a wide range of ages, ethnicities and religions. It's a protest, where its models asked: why is it so hard to live with our vulvas? In one of Mona's unisex toilet blocks, one artist group (Geltin) secreted a working toilet that enables its occupants to use a set of binoculars to obtain a close-up view of their own bowel evacuation. There is a serious question, prefaced by humour. Why is it funny to be given an opportunity to watch one's fundament at work? Why are we so ashamed of our own bodies basic natural functions? The artwork laughs at us, and we laugh along with it.

Walsh's circulating permanent collection, *Monanisms* (referencing their anxiety about collecting and showing art as somehow pretentious or 'wanky'), dominates some of the most astonishing gallery spaces. There is little or no thematic ordering, a key feature of which is that visitors simply have no idea what is coming into view next. While sexual and mortality works are well represented, many other aspects of the body find expression in the contemporary art hung in Mona, and these broaden its critical capacity. The carnivalesque emphasis on grotesque realism and the lower half of the human body by contemporary artists is also omnipresent at Mona through the work of such artists as Polly Borland, Balint Zsako, Del Kathryn Barton, Juan Davila, Wim Delvoye, Oleg Kulik, Chris Ofili and others. Many cultural theorists agree that there are historic (European and beyond) continuities in the powerful, positive and socially integrating symbolism of genitalia, excretion, fecundity and the exchange of body fluids between, and beyond, humanity. At the same time these were weaponised defiantly against authority (Webb 2005; Jervis 1999; Bakhtin 1984).

Finding themselves transported deep underground in a darkened environment, in a space that is both sexualised and grappling with death and violence in arresting and unflinching ways, is one thing. Being encouraged to drink alcohol freely once down there at a very enticing bar is another. Darkened, underground drinking is a new 'pre-liminary' art museum experiences for most people, and those who take up the offer to imbibe and see art in a less sober state, may, paradoxically, see it more productively. Taut self-control, emotional quietude and respectful solemnity, features so characteristically and long socialised in most art museum audiences are replaced with more open, receptive, and less restrained forms of engagement. Mona hoped that the experience combined excitement, emotional release (and candour) with relevant and controversial subjects that matter to contemporary audiences; where their own subjectivities are more readily drawn out, expressed and exchanged with others. We might recall that conventional museums that originally took the form of 'improving leisures', did so explicitly to wean popular culture from its love of drinking, festivity and license. That too is reversed at Mona, and by way of inculcating an interest in art.

Museum stamina

Many visitors to art museums suffer from 'museum fatigue', that feeling of mental and physical exhaustion that kicks in surprisingly quickly after spending time with art (in conventional museums). A study of Mona used the length of time people spend in its galleries as a measure of engagement with art (Franklin 2014; Franklin & Papastergiadis 2017). Museum tours are notoriously shorter than museums would ideally like them to be, though they have persuaded themselves that it's a natural and inevitable effect, similar to 'attention spans' in classrooms or churches (Davey 2005). At the Institute of Contemporary Art Boston, for example, one study found that 90 per cent of the people visited for 30 minutes or less and only 5 per cent for two hours or more (Housen 1987). Gareth Davey shows that museum fatigue (as measured for all types of museum) sets in on average at around 35–45 minutes (Davey 2005). However, in a study of over 100 exhibitions in the USA, the average time spent in them was much shorter, at only 20 minutes (Serrell 1997). At Mona 85 per cent of visitors reported staying longer than two hours and only 15 per cent less than two hours. However, 35 per cent of Mona visitors stayed in the museum for between three and five hours and a further 21 per cent spent most of the day there (Franklin & Papastergiadis 2017). It is possible to triangulate this finding against data produced by Mona's 'O' device (given to all visitors free) by calculating from elapsed time between switching it on and off. For the entire calendar year 2013, the average was 2.17 hours, or over six times the average in Serrell's study (Franklin 2014, pp. 256–257).

Some would argue that after such a long journey, visitors would inevitably want to spend more time at such a destination. But this is not the way tourism works. Typically, long distance tourists pay only fleeting attention to the most hallowed objects they travel so far to see. So, for example, Elkins (2010) reported that '... people looked at the Mona Lisa for an average of 15 seconds', while park surveys found the average time spent looking at the vastness of Grand Canyon was 17 minutes (Cross 1996).

There are three more obvious reasons why museum fatigue is less common at Mona: Mona does not tire its visitors with didactic expectations, that they are there primarily for *instruction*. Instruction requires unbroken attentiveness to an authority figure or figures, which may be all the more tiring if it is done in a dull, repetitive manner. Expecting attention to be paid to very similar artworks by the same artist is a common practice. This is avoided at Mona. Second, short attention spans may relate to the largely passive role involved in instruction. In Mona, visitors have to work under their own steam, are actively doing what they want to do from a wide menu of choices and are following their own interests and inclinations as a way into engagement with the art. Mona felt that visitors should be treated as intelligent enough and capable enough to respond to art providing the cues were not restricted to those with particular social advantages or cultural dispositions. Mona not only forces them into an active role by refusing to take an active role itself, it also provides very lively and entertaining art works in such a way that they are enlivened and entertained while they are engaged/absorbed. *Wonderment* was possibly the most important emotion that the Mona team hoped to engender in order to arouse a new, more engaged relationship between visitors, the gallery and their art. In the minds of the Mona team, wonderment was a deeply positive emotional-intellectual state that activated visitor engagement and aroused curiosity, doubt or excitement. Using a common parlance term with which to probe wonderment (according to the *Oxford Concise English Dictionary* the word 'amaze' meaning 'to fill with wonder'), a recent study asked respondents whether, when compared with other museums, their time at Mona was 'amazing'. Eighty per cent of the sample agreed with this statement, and there was no significant variation across the cohort by gender, educational background or age (Franklin & Papastergiadis 2017, p. 679).

Third, there may be something about Mona's architecture combined with its picturesque hang that involves what we might call 'pleasurable abandonment'. Individuals get lost within the museum building and lost from each other, often very quickly. Children, who are especially animated by the scale and activity of the art, typically follow their own routes, sometimes in spontaneous, same-age groups (Franklin & Sansom 2018) away from their parents. People are not only lost in space; evidently, they become lost in time.

Mona clearly hoped that their approach would engage a broader demographic than conventional museums but did it work? While the social composition of Mona's visitor profile was highly stratified and dominated by the educated middle classes, visitor experience was far less socially stratified. Thus, while 75 per cent of Mona's visitors were tertiary educated and 25 per cent non-tertiary there was little significant difference in how each group reported their overall experience there: 97 per cent of those with tertiary education said their overall experience was positive compared to 94.4 pe cent of the non-tertiary educated. Equally, 80.3 per cent of the tertiary educated agreed with the statement 'Visiting Mona has made me think about a lot of things' as compared with 79 per cent of the non-tertiary educated; while 82 per cent of the tertiary educated agreed with the statement 'My visit to Mona has enriched my life' compared with 73.8 per cent of the non-tertiary educated (Franklin & Papastergiadis 2017, pp. 9–10).

Conclusion: festivity within and beyond the museum walls

We have already seen at the New Museum and PS1 how anti-museums are often activists, 'a practice in which some element of the art takes place in the 'outside world' (Wallis 2017, p. 139). Mona insisted from the beginning on the socially transformative aspirations of the contemporary art it collected and on the socially transformative power of ritual and festivity in all human societies. It used the festive register as a key method of activism (and activation). Arguably Mona has been studied in greater depth than the other case studies and such aspirations have been empirically investigated.

Mona rendered the museum into a carnivalesque space where the concepts of pilgrimage (travelling so far to see art), liminality (though topsy-turvy upending and reversal of everyday spaces, normative museum practices, hierarchy and expectations) and humour (at the expense of authority) were mobilised forcefully. However, from the beginning, in its original museum aims of 2007, it laid out a role for itself beyond its museum walls (Fraser 2013):

- Improvement to cultural facilities in Tasmania.
- Cross-branding with Moorilla.
- Educational facility for schools.
- Academic resource and research facility.
- Creative environment for artists/writers in residence.
- Patronage of contemporary arts and culture.
- Self-marketing: sufficient generator of controversy to continually engage media attention.
- Put a rocket up public collections/ generate Government interest in community driven projects with possible funding outcomes.

All of these came into being in some way but spectacularly in the case of the very last element. Even before they rolled out the new museum, they deployed the festive register at a summer festival, that extended throughout the city of Hobart (*Mona Foma*), and in 2013 they combined with local arts organisations and the city council to create a mid-winter festival (*Dark Mofo*) to celebrate the dark, cold depths of winter and to welcome the new sun.

The Christian colonial history of Hobart, and its adherence to the Christian ritual calendar had been diametrically out of sync with the seasons of the Southern Hemisphere, leaving the coming of the new sun, new life, and a new year unrecognised ritually as it has always been in the Northern Hemisphere – as a time of renewal, rebirth, and redemption. Winter festivals in the European tradition, particularly carnival, became associated with the presence, continuity, and indefatigability of local communities in their landscapes, where their collective body was expressed by an exuberant emphasis on the corporeal body, often in giant, fecund forms and in promiscuous association with their environment and nature, with an emphasis on the lower half of the body. Powered by Walsh's patronage, clowning and considerable ability to source exciting contemporary art, their mid-winter festival restored the historic connections between art,

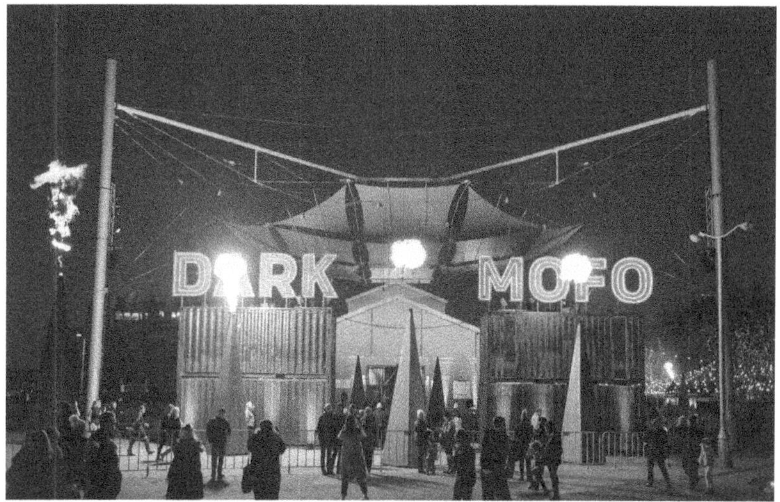

Figure 5.5 Entry to Dark Mofo

Photo credit: Dark Mofo/Rémi Chauvin, Image courtesy Dark Mofo, Hobart, Tasmania, Australia 2018

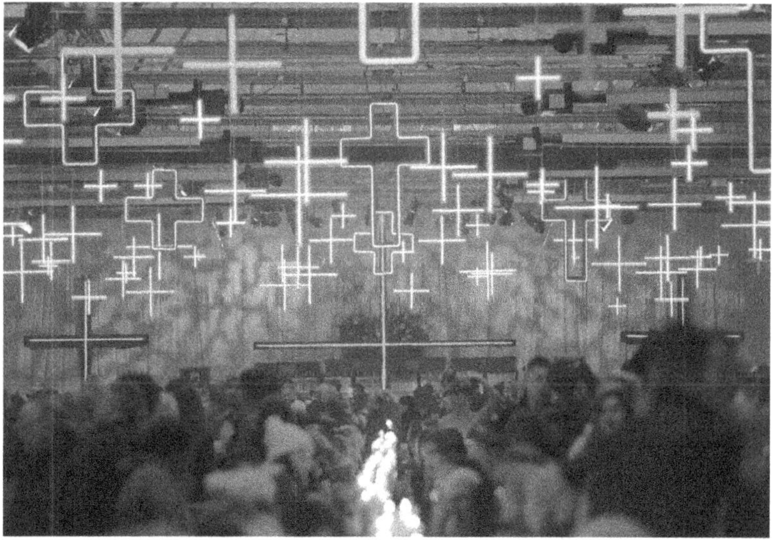

Figure 5.6 Dark Mofo, City of Hobart Winter Feast

Photo credit: Dark Mofo/Jesse Hunniford Image courtesy Dark Mofo, Hobart, Tasmania, Australia

ritual, season, nature, emotion at the so-called the borderline 'between art and life' (Bakhtin 1984, p. 8). Dark Mofo extended the tourist season into a long winter period and at a time when its residents were mostly present (they were largely visitors elsewhere during the summer). With a vibrant winter season there was now sufficient cultural activity to support a new ancillary ring of youthful arts, cultural and especially food and drink businesses that had never taken root or lasted very long before (McGarry 2018). The city filled with visitors as never before, because now it was a fast-changing and hip place that attracted artists and cultural makers as well as bands and artists wishing to be included in Mona's art festival line-ups.

In 2013 Lonely Planet ranked Hobart the 7th best city in the world and in doing so it lionised Mona, citing it as the main catalyst for Hobart's extraordinary cultural florescence. In 2015, Lonely Planet ranked Mona the 20th best place in the world and Mona the best art gallery in the world (Ikin 2015). Hitherto, according to the Lonely Planet story, Hobart had been a 'sleepy harbour town' that had attracted a solid 'outdoorsy' set to its pristine natural wilderness and coastline. At another level, the artists and a significant cross section of interstate and overseas hipster plus art world culture was a spectacle in its own right and provided local people with a compelling reason to sample the world's best contemporary art with them. Across France only 13 per cent of the population attended a museum of contemporary in 2013 (Bigot et al. 2013), but in Hobart 82 per cent of tertiary educated and 65 per cent non-tertiary educated residents attended Dark Mofo, with more attending in subsequent years. At the mothership museum, Mona attracted a majority of residents from both local cities. About 75 per cent of the people of Hobart and 63 per cent of the people of Glenorchy had been at least once to Mona in the previous year. Over 25 per cent of Hobartians and over 20 per cent of Glenorchians had been more than twice (Franklin 2018).

If anti-museums are responses to critiques of the conventional modern art museum, then arguably Mona is surely one of the most explicitly thought through and enacted examples of its kind. It is unique, yet it does have things in common with other anti-museums. Its darkened gallery spaces and theatrical lighting is similar to the scenography at La Collection de l'Art Brut and it, too, champions non-academic art and art that conventional museums refuse or censor. Both museums derive from the collections of just one person, and, in both cases, they were determined and well-resourced individuals capable of inspiring talented, courageous teams of collaborators. Walsh and Judd on the other hand were both keen builders, Judd building a museum from large numbers of abandoned building and Walsh building new. Walsh instructed his architect not to compete with the art. Judd tied his art work, his art practice, his collection and his installations into the life of existing buildings. Both broke down the symbolic association between art, power and authority and imposing powerful buildings. In this regard PS1 and New Museum and Mona were similar in that they all engaged their communities and art publics by moving outside the museum walls in a tangible and committed way, occupying public space as a way of extending their relevance to the life of their cities. PS1 and Mona connected visual art with music very successfully, using music that people knew to introduce them to visual art that they didn't (Ritchie 2011).

In the next chapter, we encounter in Paris an anti-museum that went the opposite direction way. It took street art from its natural habitat in public spaces and objects into a building that was, and was not, a museum; it was both a private and a public space; both an everyday space and an extraordinary space. In other words, yet another iteration of the anti-museum.

6 Art42, Paris

Introduction

One of the distinguishing features of anti-museum variants is the impossibility of knowing what to expect in advance of visiting them for the first time. They are also more of a challenge to find. They seldom hang out in the same inner-city cultural precincts favoured by conventional institutions, and Art42 is no exception here. It is situated at a safe distance from the 1st Arrondissement (home to the Louvre, Opera House, Le Centre Pompidou and the Musée des Arts Décoratifs), in the outer northern 17th Arrondissement, close to the now-trendy Batignolles neighbourhood. Even so, my ill-advised walk from Les Halles on a freezing cold, wet March night via Rue de Rivoli, Avenue de l'Opéra and the long slog up Rue de Clichy to the ring road at Boulevard des Maréchaux was pretty grim in places. This chapter investigates the youngest of the anti-museums in this book. Established in 2016, it has the lightest material footprint of them all, which seems appropriate given that it is a museum of street art that champions its sparing and ephemeral presence in public spaces. Yet, as a form for outsider/activist art there are interesting parallels with the Collection de l'Art Brut, and the New Museum. It provides something of a model for affordable and flexible museum arrangements that many forms of emerging art and artists could emulate.

Being relatively new on the Paris art scene there was not a great deal of information available about Art42, and their website gave very little away. In fact, apart from a list of list of prominent street artists featured in their collection, there were absolutely no grand claims, self-descriptions, motherhood statements or aspirations littering their site. In an interview, its collector–owner, Nicolas Laugero Lasserre, thought he had invented the anti-museum concept, and was genuinely surprised it was a well-established critical concept in art history, and a thing about which a book was being

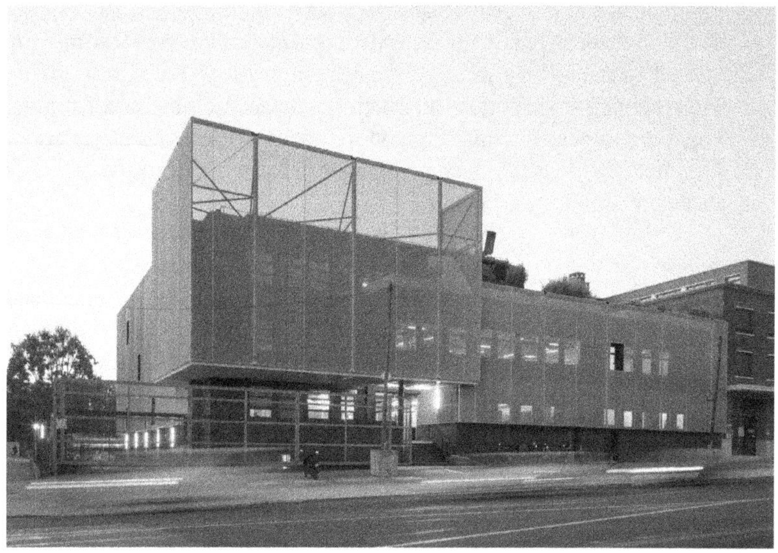

Figure 6.1 École 42, Paris

Source: Courtesy Art42

written. Again, as we saw in the case of Mona, it was not necessary to know the centuries-old discourse on anti-museums for it to make perfect sense to contemporary museum makers/reformers.

Arriving at its address at 96 Boulevard Bessières, one sees no evidence of a museum: there is no sign, no grand portico. The building it occupies is not an art institution, but a high school. It's no ordinary school though: it's École 42. As the *New York Times* states,

> legions of tech entrepreneurs, CEOs and ministers have been drawn to the unorthodox methods applied in École 42, poles apart from the government-run education system. There are no teachers and no classes, only group projects, and students roam around free, day and night, seven days a week.
>
> (Morenne 2016)

Instead, students learn from each other as they jointly work their way through several demanding levels of computer programming/coding. According to École 42, USA, their new scion in Silicon Valley, California,

> the students are the ones in charge of their success and that of their classmates, and it is centred around a curriculum which is 100% practical and project based. In order to progress on the projects that are offered to them, they must rely on the strength of the group, giving and receiving information, alternating between training and learning. This peer-to-peer learning method, removes the subordinate relationship of students. Each student is responsible for a part of the project's success within the group.
>
> (www.42.us.org/program/peer-to-peer-learning/)

There is something strikingly familiar in the language of this school and the way David Walsh talked about Mona. The language of instruction has been removed in order to augment a less passive pedagogic experience. École 42 is a tuition-free, unconventional computer academy founded with €70 million by the telecom mogul Xavier Niel in 2013. A former hacker, he was the first to set up a French internet provider and has netted a fortune of US$6.1 billion. Niel puts his success down to the unconventional ways he acquired his core skills and believed it could be cultivated in new forms of learning culture.

In turn, Niel was approached by Nicolas Laugero Lasserre (an equally unconventional collector of street art, and Director of ICART, a Parisian art management school) with an idea to locate his collection across the entire École 42 building, as an exhibitionary platform. As with many significant collectors, Laugero Lasserre believed his collection should always be available to be seen by the public; street art especially. He had already turned his hand to exhibiting extensively across France, innovating new ways to use unconventional spaces that retained/widened some of the qualities of the street which the art was intended for. Now he was seeking a permanent place close to his home.

At the same time, he deployed École 42's method by giving the students of ICART and École 42 the opportunity to organise and provide guided tours to a wider public. As Morenne (2016, p. 2) argued:

> Art42 is as far from a museum as École 42 is from a school, starting with its name, which was derived from book *The Hitchhiker's Guide to the Galaxy*, where the number 42 is 'the answer to life, the universe and everything.'

A tour of Art42

Art42's website was produced by its student organisers and it was they who had booked me in for an evening tour of the collection. Impressively,

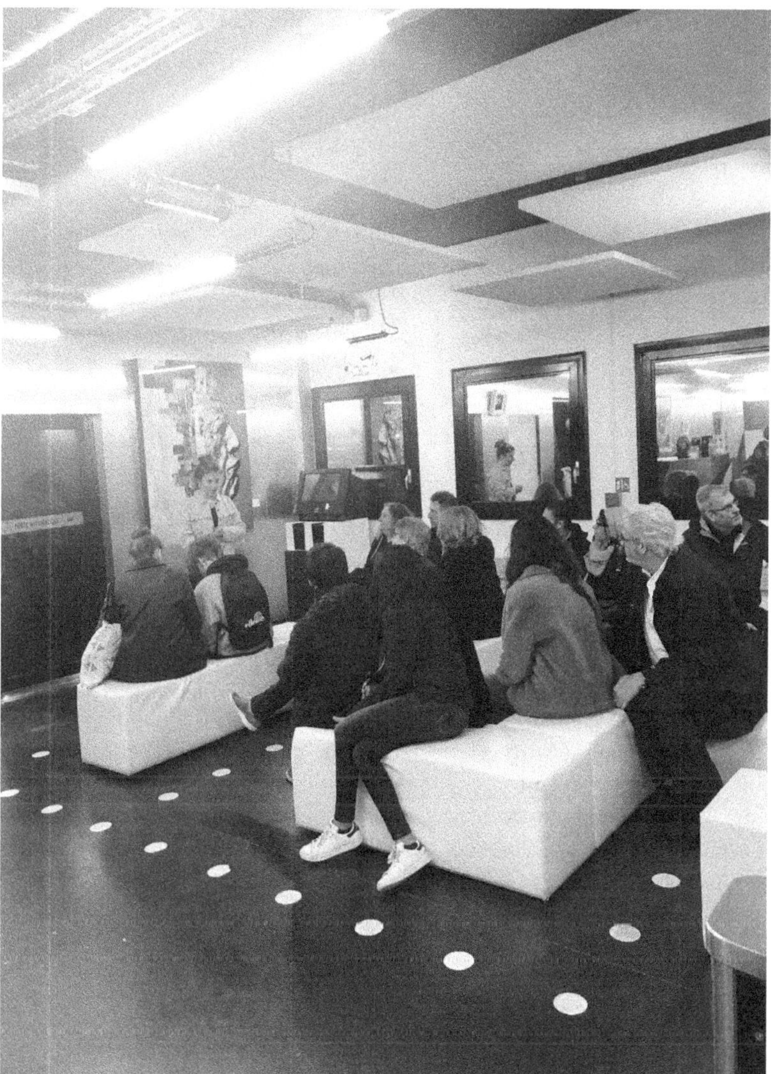

Figure 6.2 Assembled tour group

Photo: Adrian Franklin

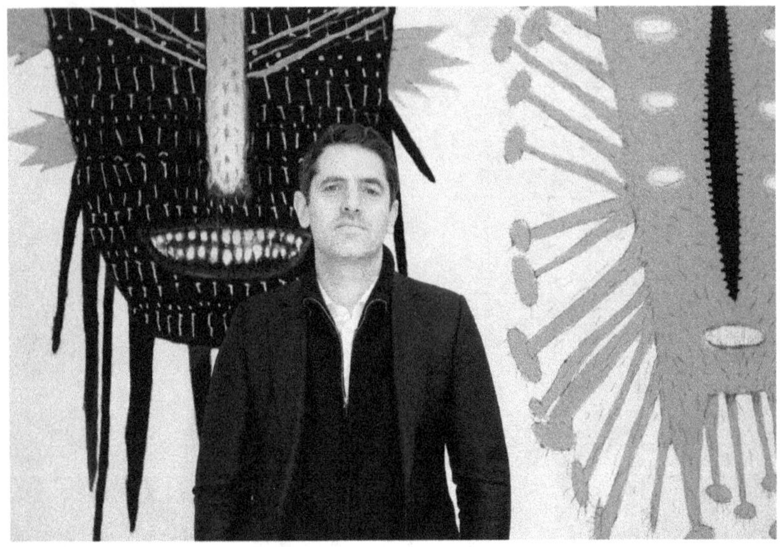

Figure 6.3 Portrait Nicolas Laugero Lasserre
© Alexandra Baboneau (3)

they organised tours in French and English. Entering the building one had to traverse high security electronic gates, built to protect the buildings massive endowment of computing technology. Once inside its light and airy lobby, a large crowd of visitors were being processed, organised and seated into three or four groups awaiting the commencement of the next volley of evening tours. I was surprised to find the place completely packed out with visitors of all ages, from all over the world. The students in charge of front of house operations were all in their late teens and early twenties, they were very welcoming, enthusiastic and well organised.

There were no security staff, no curatorial staff, no signs or directions just a very low key, hands-on help from makeshift desks with plenty of other helpers on hand. As we waited for our guides to complete their prior tour, we could take in some impressive works of art that were hung in the lobby: by Invader [*Invasion Kit*]; a larger piece by JR [*The Wrinkles of the City, Los Angeles – Robert Upside Down, Downtown USA*] and a small but exquisite stencilled painting by Stew. All of them were recognisable big 'names', either hung in an unassuming way in everyday spaces of the building or painted directly onto its surfaces as site-specific works. From every doorway and corridor leading away from us we could see much more art in the connecting spaces of the building. Well, there had to be, we had signed up for a *two-hour* tour.

The ease and informality, alongside the outstanding art and the general state of surprise and delight among the tour groups broke down the social distance between everyone as they sat waiting for their tours to start. I noted the noise in the lobby, it was the deafening sound of excited people. It was a refreshing, laid-back occasion that no one was quite ready for. We were in a new kind of museum being treated as adults by staff young enough to be our children, grandchildren or friends.

The Loan tour

Before too long Loan made herself known to us as our guide for the tour. I assumed she was an artist herself and had adopted a single word moniker. A Belgian by birth, she was a confident 20-year-old with impeccable English. In her groups there were English speakers from all corners of the globe. She introduced herself in the following way:

> I'm an art and culture student and my headmaster is big fan of street art and he's been meaning to make a museum for some time. I think it was about three years ago he got talking with the Director from this school who offered to allow him to put his artworks around his school and, just make a partnership between our two worlds, I guess. The museum opened in 2016 and we the students are in charge of it, so we do the visits for extra credit and we got to learn about street art, which is very cool. Sometimes we have exchange programs between our two schools, so some students from here [École 42] also do the tours, sometimes they actually know more about the artwork than we do.
>
> It's very cool. It's like some kind of an anti-museum – actually, this is the only museum devoted to street art in France and I like to say this because I don't really like the way French people think! We have that reputation to be the country of art and culture, but in Germany and in England they've been opening street art museums all over for maybe 20 years and this is the first one and it only opened last year.

We then moved to the first of the artworks that Loan wanted to talk about, *No artists tolerate reality* (2016) by VLP (France). This was made when the museum opened and will only fit the specific space where it was made. She tells us that it was inspired by a group of Islamic women who were photographed holding signs saying: 'Not in my Name'. Then, we stopped to view another work on a pillar but our eyes instantly alighted on the vast space opening up on our left, a room full of Mac computers with groups of students working together at different points along each row, some deep in thought others in lively conversations, others laughing.

That this is a workspace, and one open to the public, coupled with the fact that it is an informal space in which a great range of social transactions take place outside the official oversight of authorities, means that people who occupy the building are not here first, or specifically, to see or consume art. Because the art in École 42 is both incidental and ubiquitous in its public manifestation, it is not unlike a street or other urban space in its apprehension. Equally, while we the visitors do come here to see the art, we do so not in a hived off, aesthetic, rarefied art institution, but in the everyday work space of others, *while they work*. It is not a space managed and disciplined so that we may perform the task of taking in instruction. The building was not designed as an attractive and aesthetic space in its own right or with a specific remit to exhibit art, but, like loft museums that reused abandoned factories, workshops and warehouses, this basic school building is also 'simple, flexible and egoless' (McClellan 2008, pp. 93–97). And, like loft museums, which emulate 'the spaces in which their contents were made' (the loft-like studios of trained and recognised artists), it transcends the usual commercial, political and aesthetic associations of the art museum to achieve a kind of original purity' – after all, school buildings are part or the urban streetscape as much as anything else (McClellan 2008, p. 98). Shortly after our ground floor tour Loan took us outside to the rear of the building, where the self-taught artist Romain Froquet, had painted a massive abstract mural (*Art42 2016*) a few days before Art42 opened. It is based on a Japanese road system taken from Google Maps. The wall it covered would have created a dark, shady area in the school grounds but with the luminous Froquet piece there, blue, red and pink hues shine out to brighten the rear of the building. Froquet has specialised in precisely these projects in an attempt to illuminate, activate and bring new joy to gloomy urban backwaters (Gzeley 2017). Other artists, notably the stencil makers MonkeyBird, collude with the darkness and shade and we are soon aware that Nicolas Laugero Lasserre's collection of MonkeyBird, with whom he has a special relationship, are scattered throughout the building. These artists effect an impressive juxtaposition in the nether regions of the school at night.

Returning to the main block, Loan took the group to the first floor of the building and a journey through some 80 works of art. She chose works that were interesting to her and skilfully told us why she liked them, and what she knew about the artist, their aspirations, styles and character but also, how they act within the cultural ecologies of cities and specific kinds of urban space and society. This was not art history as the main take home

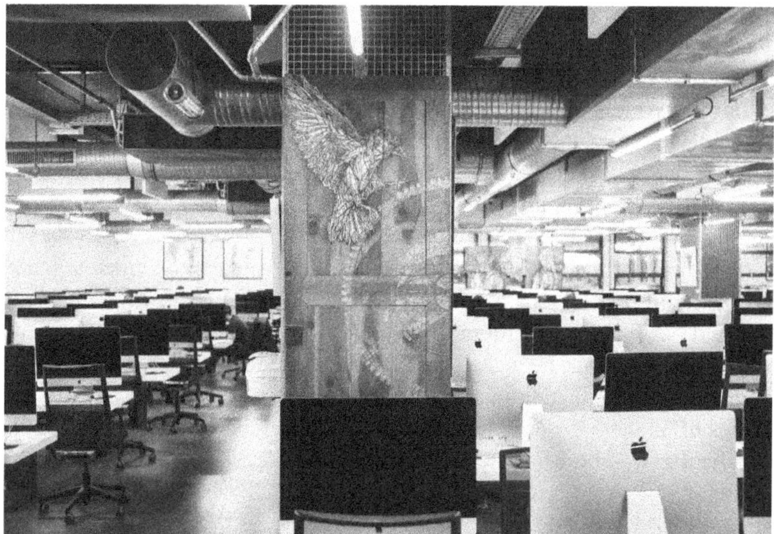

Figure 6.4 MonkeyBird at Art42

Photo: © Frederic Deval-Mairie de Bordeaux

message but a narrative about art, artists and the impact it has on urban life.

In her tours, Loan favours single works to talk about rather than the collection of works of specific artists, always a mixture of artist biography with personal comments and relationships that the artists have created with the museum and its collector. Thus, we were spared dates and periods and the repetition that often makes guided tours dull. Once we had had an introduction to some 25 works on the first main floor, the tour style changed. On subsequent floors, we were simply left to view the art on our own, and Loan was happy to take questions during and after the viewing. This was also the way it was done at the Chinati and Judd foundations in Marfa, Texas. Our two hours passed briskly and pleasurably and the visitors were visibly animated and excited by their experience.

Art42 collector: Nicolas Laugero Lassere

I met Nicolas in late August 2018 at Café Victoria in Rue Pierre Charron, a smart Parisian street just off Avenue des Champs-Élysées, opposite ICART (L'école du management de la culture et du marché de l'art), where he is Director. He is a youthful, energetic and passionate 43-year-old who has achieved a great deal, both inside and outside the art world of Paris and across France. Like David Walsh, he grew up in a modest family largely devoid of art or art experiences. He is emphatic about the tragedy of an art world that failed so many working-class French people – and a sizeable chunk of the middle classes too. He mentions that 80 per cent of the French population grow up with no art in their homes and with no memories of visiting art galleries. And like David Walsh, his passion and drive was critical to the establishment of an anti-museum. Knowing the potential value that art plays in the life of individuals and cities twinned with the difficulty of persuading more people to enter art museums, has spurred Nicolas to place more art in alternative exhibitionary spaces of the everyday. However, he is also keenly aware that he only came to be active in the art world by a rare and particularly unusual series of accidents and twists of fate.

Nicolas was born in Nice and grew up in Marseille. He left for Paris aged 20.

> When I arrived in Paris I knew nothing about art, but I began to learn. At the age of 20 I was born into a cultural environment! I realised that it's important to open the spirit to it, to develop tolerance. You know, culture and arts can change your world. It's easy to say, but it's true. All artists have vision, which they can share and we, non-artists, can bring something different to it too.
>
> After that I had chance to meet with the artists. Around 1995–97 I got to know a few artists who lived in the squats close by. I began to discover an underground universe and I was fascinated. I felt I had the same sensibility as them … their spirits seduced me and I wanted to be a part of their world. I began to collect their work, very modestly, 50 Euro, 100 Euro pieces – because I had no money. I was buying directly from the artists and one day I bought something a lot more expensive like 300 Euros, I was 23 or so. So, that was Miss.Tic, my first piece. She's famous because she started in the 1980s and is one of the founders of street art in France.

In 1995, when Nicolas arrived in Paris he started out in press relations. When he was 24, he began working as a press officer for *Espace Cardin*, formerly the Café des Ambassadeurs, a theatre, arts and exhibition space at the Theatre de la Ville, near Place de la Concorde. Under Pierre Cardin's direction it was a new form of arts and performance space with theatre, ballet, dance, exhibitions, fashion shows, cinema and conferences. Nicolas branched into administration becoming Deputy Director and, in

2006 aged 31, its Director – overseeing substantial renovations. For ten years, he was in the perfect place to learn about the art world and the exhibition of art and from around 2008 he began to exhibit his growing collection across France. When *Espace Cardin* closed in 2015, he moved to be Director of ICART (School of Management of Culture and Art Market) where he had been teaching students for some time.

Seemingly, in everything he has done, he stayed faithful to his roots in street art, not only by continuing to collect it, working with street artists and exhibiting his collection, but by promoting street art, artists and the cultural life of urban France. Even as a Director of a college, preparing students to enter the art market as administrators of galleries, art museums, auction houses etc., he is mindful of how art is more significant than the market alone and how his students need to appreciate this.

From temporary exhibitions to a ~~museum~~

Inevitably, a true fan of street art will feel uneasy about hoarding it away in private, even if it has been sold or given away as a drawing or print. Thus, there is a built-in imperative to find ways to exhibit it publicly, to keep it in the public eye and exhibited raw (i.e. without overlay or mediation).

While street art diffuses into popular consciousness spontaneously, its more formal exhibition establishes it as 'art', on an equal footing with 'recognised artists' and 'art'. For Nicolas, it seemed churlish not to enable this capacity to be realised.

Since most collections will eventually pose practical and spatial problems of storage, keeping it on the move through exhibitions is something of a solution to several issues. Keeping such a collection in an appropriate form of exhibitionary life, in circulation and on view is often deemed the ideal solution. But how does someone with a modest income do this?

Nicolas's experience at *Espace Cardin* assisted him in locating and organising some 40 exhibitionary platforms across a variety of novel spaces in cities and towns. Starting in 2008, it was done largely at his own expense and by 2012 he was getting tired of the hard, if rewarding, work it entailed. In the beginning, he had 80 pieces but the collection grew to around 300. Such intensive exhibition work changed the nature of his collecting style. Small works were the feature of his early collection but it became apparent that larger works worked better for shows, or at least there had to be a significant proportion of large works. Thus, he concentrated more on acquiring larger works as well as getting artists to do some in situ, temporary works. While more successful, the larger works were harder to manage logistically.

The only way to step off the travelling treadmill was to find a suitable permanent venue – but to be suitable it also had to be free. In 2013, the opening of École 42 was attracting massive attention from the press and other media. Nicolas approached them with a plan to offer his collection to the school free, as an apt, inspiring and energising embellishment to their already vibrant culture. To his surprise they were keen on the idea and so began the massive task of hanging the collection across the spaces of a school. Nicolas liked the idea that his collection would be seen constantly by changing cohorts of students, but he was also able to add further public and pedagogical value by training his own students to run the collection as a museum accessible to the general public through tours that they would organise and run. Here we might note the extension of trust to people other than accredited experts in the anti-museums featured in this volume (i.e. to visitors, students and artists) and its positive impact.

With the bulk of the collection safely hung as Art42, Nicolas was able to look for other feasible opportunities. He continued to curate new exhibitions, which had the added attraction of circulating and refreshing the hang at Art42. Recently, for example, he curated the show Légendes Urbaines at the breath-taking underground space of a World War II submarine base in Bordeaux. Built by the occupying Germans in 1942, and still structurally intact, it is a darkly lit Bond villain lair, complete with labyrinthine chambers and deep-water basins.

More ambitious still is the extension of Art42 into new external exhibitionary platforms, reaching new and varied forms of public space. For example, as a contribution to the project 'Réinventer La Seine' (Reinvent the Seine), Nicolas collaborated with Géraud Boursin and Eric Philippon and with *Seine Design* to design and build *Fluctuart*, the world's first floating urban art centre in Paris. Opened in spring 2019, at the foot of the Pont des Invalides and facing the Grand Palais, *Fluctuart* is entirely dedicated to street art and embedding it in the local community. The 1000-metre-square space will span three storeys and comprise: a permanent exhibition of street art's greatest names; a cafe and bar; a springboard gallery (which aims to launch new artists into post-study practice) in the hold; participation in cultural events such as urban art fairs; funding artists' residences in some of the units of the building; providing premises for the cultural association *Artistik Rezo*; offering creative and educational workshops for young people; maintaining a library with specialised books and making the building available to hire for cultural or private events (Sortiraparis 2019).

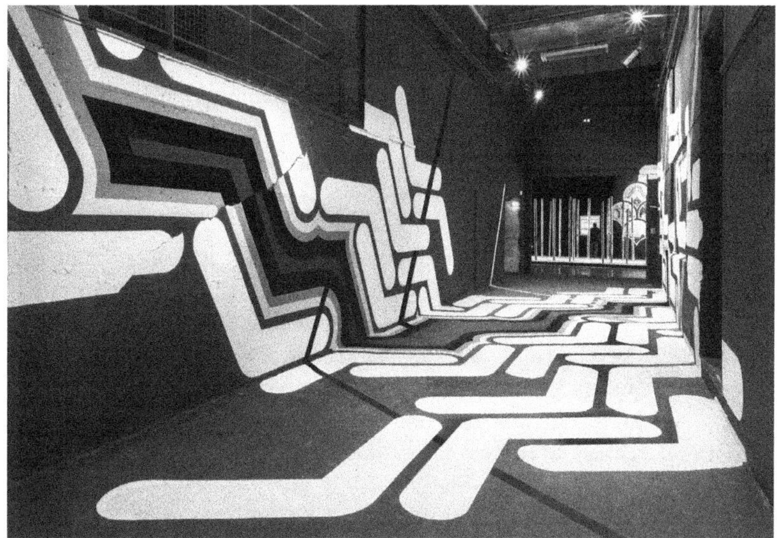

Figure 6.5 Erell at Légendes Urbaines

Photo: © Frederic Deval- Mairie de Bordeaux

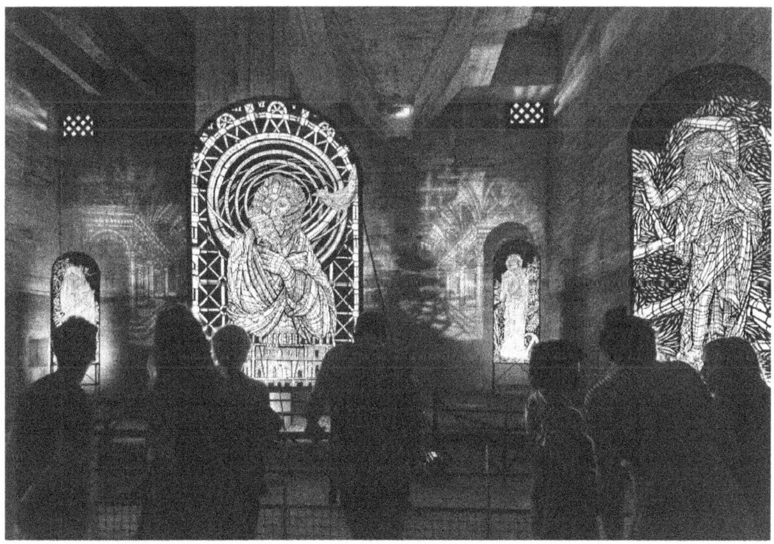

Figure 6.6 Romain Froquet at Légendes Urbaines

Photo: © Frederic Deval-Mairie de Bordeaux

Conclusion

It is as a passionate insider activist that Nicolas created his collection of street art and his numerous exhibitions across France. In this sense, he is also a cultural intermediary, simultaneously extending the reach of street art to more people and places (Iniesta 2016, p. 13, O'Connor 1999). As Iniesta argues, it was as a militant that he conceived Art42, and identified a tangible problem worth addressing:

> There is a generation gap between [official art] institutions and urban art. Curators of these institutions confined the street art movement to forms of street expression, *to popular culture* without seeing its diversity, currents and aesthetics. Street artists play with situations, objects and urban settings, using poetry and provocation. So, we must integrate new uses and disrupt the very notion of a museum. It is necessary to respect the characteristics of street art, to adapt to it, to its codes.
>
> (Iniesta 2016, p. 13)

Art42 does this in two ways. First, it is a museum without being one in the conventional sense since it is a school, and a rebel school at that, which breaks with normative codes of didacticism. Significantly, it is placed in the everyday spaces of the school and is only encountered as an incidental backcloth, unrelated to the business at hand for its students. As with street art, they encounter it in the course of their lives rather than being directed to it, or even choosing to have it in their lives. It comes and goes as the hang is adjusted, added to or borrowed for external exhibitions. It was inserted into their lifeworld through the agency of an outsider, a street art collector who identifies with its aesthetic and its line of flight. But then they were invited to participate in the social life of the collection as a new form of museum.

Second, it is not like a conventional museum in being a private collection of just one person and ordered without professionally trained curatorial staff. There are plenty of public one-person collector museums, including the very first one built by John Tradescant the Elder in London, whose eclectic collection of wonders was inherited by Elias Ashmole and formed a major part of what became the Ashmolean Museum at Oxford, the first collection ever to be called a museum. Others, such as the Frick, the Whitney, The Wallace Collection and The Soanes Museum mostly comprise art, or the decorative and architectural arts. However, Art42 departs from them all in the sense that it is not conventionally curated and governed by museum professionals but by an amateur collector-insider and a constant stream of student cohorts connecting with significant flows of visitors nationally and internationally.

As an extraordinarily rich and living collection that is refreshed so often from externally mobile exhibitionary platforms, Art42 has become a valued and vibrant museum concept. Its enthusiastic youthful student organisers are fans of the art rather than its guardians, and closer culturally to the street culture of their artists than professional museum curators. Much of the work is donated by artists either as in situ works, installations or framed drawings and paintings; and in that sense they have a powerful stake and role in how the museum looks and works. Yet this is also part of these students training as art world professions and one gains the impression that they will take in the anti-museum concept and seed it more widely than is currently the case.

Art42 is similar to PS1, New York, in that it also inhabits a school building where artists work and install their own art. Yet it is just as eccentric as the other anti-museums considered in this volume, and enacted through the will of one person taking advantage of unique sets of personal circumstances and responding to the affordances of very particular localities. The absence of these properties in the emerging modern museum was precisely what the earliest critics railed against, and why they saw them as lifeless mausoleums. Art42 is full of life with all the messiness and contingency that authenticates it as embedded, connected and evolving, and in the true spirit of art (Rorty 1989; Zukin 2010).

7 Conclusion

The art of museums beyond convention

Through six detailed case studies from the USA, Europe and Australia, it has been shown how the 'anti-museum critique', detailed in the introduction, has been realised and operationalised in many vibrant, experimental and sustained ways, resulting in the formation of new museum-like institutions that embody some or all anti-museum aims and values.

It has been shown, that while opposing the highly standardised form of conventional art museums, these examples of anti-museums do not constitute a unified, binary opposite. Instead the anti-museum idea opens up a multiplicity of possible alternatives and variations where even holding to one shape or set of museum aims is contingent on the shifting cultural ecologies and art world conjunctures that they specifically aim to be a constituent part of. It is by submitting to emergent ecological connections and conditions, and being embedded within them, rather than standing alone as an external authority figure, that they have altered the exhibitionary complex away from one dominated by the 'modern museum'. And it is by shifting their focus from the nationalistic, corporate and academic interests and foci of conventional museums to alliances with contemporary artists and what John Roberts (2015, p. 130) called their emergent neo-avant-gardiste cultural critique in the mid-twentieth century, that more localised and locally engaged forms of anti-museums made sense and were founded and thrived. Thus, they became part of artistic–political practice and broke with the conventional museum as an institution of cultural political governance. A summary of their achieved changes, as discussed in this book, are given in Table 7.1 below.

Forceful founders

It has been shown how the anti-museums featured in this book have been developed and driven by very strong, charismatic personalities including artists (Dubuffet in the case of La Collection de l'Art Brut; Judd in the case

Table 7.1 Points of comparison between conventional art museums and anti-museums – summary table

Conventional art museum	*Anti-museums*	*Examples*
Standardised/professional /accredited/general/ anthology	Niched/amateur, particular, responsive to its own art ecology	CDLAB; New Museum, PS1, Judd, Art42
Spatial location in social centre	Spatial location on social margin/periphery	CDLAB; Judd, Mona
Relatively fixed and stable structure	Experimental/fluid	CDLAB; New Museum; PS1; Judd; Art42; Mona
Taste, connoisseurship, social distinction, anointed artist	Cultural specificity, social inclusion, diversity, art by all	CDLAB; New Museum; PS1; Judd; Mona; Art42
Assembly (museum disconnected from places and contexts of art making)	Assemblage (anti-museums connected to places of making and social contexts)	CDLAB; New Museum; PS1; Judd; Art42 (Mona in part)
Art history focus	Artist focus	CDLAB; New Museum; PS1; Judd; Art42; Mona
Art consumption	Art production, extension	CDLAB; New Museum; PS1; Judd; Art42; Mona
Instruction (tell)	Engagement, immersion, trust (show)	CDLAB; New Museum; PS1; Judd; Art42; Mona
Serious	Relaxed, not serious, humour, satirical, mocking	CDLAB; New Museum; PS1; Judd; Art42; Mona
Emotionally neutral/ anaesthetised	Emotionally heightened	CDLAB; New Museum; PS1; Judd; Art42; Mona
Academic	Activist	CDLAB; New Museum; Art42; Mona
Formal	Informal (to radically informal)	CDLAB; New Museum; PS1; Judd; Art42; Mona
Public need guidance	Public need trust, encouragement and opportunity	CDLAB; New Museum; PS1; Judd; Art42; Mona
Grand architectures	Vernacular, reused, modest housing	CDLAB; PS1; Judd; Art42; (New Museum; Mona in part)
Legal–rational authority (political, commercial, collectors, academics)	Charismatic leadership, (rebels, outsiders, artists, collectors, curators)	CDLAB; New Museum; PS1; Judd; Art42; Mona

of Chinati and Judd Foundations), artist-orientated collectors (Walsh in the case of Mona; Brett in the case of Museum of Everything; Laugero Lassere in the case of Art42) and curators (Heiss in the case of PS1 and Tucker in the case of the New Museum). Almost all of the founders were autodidact amateur exhibitors and only Tucker was professionally trained, though many later directors and staff recruited to them were professionally trained. All of the founders had become disenchanted by the conventional art museum as it was configured within significant aspects of the art world – or what has been called the extended exhibitionary complex (Bennett 1988; Lorente 2011, 2016; Smith 2009, 2012). In many instances, these forceful individuals were able to create and command new sources of funding and exhibitionary platforms/spaces, often on the social margins. In many cases, we can identify these anti-museums with the arrival of new forms of art, with art brut, contemporary art and street art, all of them outsiders to the conventional art museum initially. The ascendance of contemporary art resulted in the clash of aims between living artists wishing to have their art properly and fully engaged with their publics and conventional art museums oriented more to their collections, art history and didactic educational programmes. In the first instance, new forms of art and artists were often championed by these individuals, often using ingenious means to obtain spaces for their work and exhibition (e.g. Judd's Marfa; PS1; New Museum; Art42). After 2000, the rise of prominent contemporary artists and their collectors (often in tandem), and their spectacular command of financial resources, gave them considerable powers to find or create alternative exhibitionary strategies (Mona; Art42) (Franklin 2020).

Beyond convention: experiment and flux

Through participant observation of anti-museum tours in these institutions, it became clear that they are visited by many working in the cultural and creative industries for whom they represent an invaluable pool of rethinking and experimentation with new iterations of the art museum. Most of these anti-museums are sites of disturbance that emanate from the forms of art they exhibit, the artists who continually create new art and art forms and the visitors whose changing worlds and subjectivities they are sensitive to. In this way, anti-museums do not set themselves up as sources of authority that force artists and art public to respond to them in a hierarchical fashion. Rather, they respond to and work alongside artists and their publics and often their wider communities as more democratic formations. They also foster less hierarchical connections with children, avoiding hived off children's educational sections, for example. I formed the view that children experienced easy-going and pleasurable forms of engagement with them, and while that remains to be studied further, I have made a start on that at Mona with Michelle Sansom in 2018.

Making history

Anti-museums therefore avoid didacticism and didactic products, preferring to participate more directly in the socially transformative currents of art and society, connecting artists with their publics and becoming a public space for the contagion and dialogue of new ideas. As the New Museum's Director Lisa Phillips (2017, p. 9) remarked, 'they are not a place for preserving and recording history, but a place where history is made'. This makes all of them exciting places to visit because they are engaged in the dynamic and changing relationships between artists, civil society and place. Arguably, the conventional museum created the very disposition to art history that limited their appeal to the educated middle classes, as well as limiting what museums could do. By being more politically, culturally, socially and publicly facing, active and embedded spatially, many of these anti-museums have created new and embryonic art publics among those that had remained relative strangers to the conventional art museums (Prior 2002).

Rare: but for how long?

While it is possible to conclude that they are all mostly successful interventions in the art world, it is nonetheless true that they are comparative rarities. Why is this? Globally, the potency of contemporary art is recognised by political power through its willingness and capacities to limit it and suppress it, financially, ideologically and politically. While it is often considered a dangerous loose cannon by some nations and heavily suppressed, even in the liberal West it has been corralled within highly conventional institutions where a degree of political regulation prevents it from being the critical force it aspires to be. It is not at all surprising that contemporary neo-liberal/populist governments have cut funding and sought to take a more direct role in the distribution of funds within the 'national interest'. Museum boards were always historically dominated by bankers, industrialists, politicians and moral entrepreneurs whose historic role has been to organise funding for building, acquisition and exhibition as well as maintain its civilising mission (Rentschler 2015). By being publicly funded they are required to avoid overt political bias or moral outrage, which often means politically neutralising the art it might otherwise aspire to exhibit. In numerous cases, we have seen how art has not only been neutered, but subject to moral witch hunts and censorship – even when the official moral regulators have deemed it as benign, as in the Bill Henson case documented by David Marr (2008). In 2011 David Walsh, owner of Mona, produced an anti-museum to challenge what David Marr (2008, p. 58) feared might become 'an unpresented purge of the art world', by which he meant contemporary art.

Historically most art museums around the world rely heavily on the patronage of wealthy collectors of art and it may well be, paradoxically, that among the growing numbers of rich art collectors of contemporary art, more will follow the example of David Walsh, James Brett and Nicolas Laugero Lassere, by building their own museums rather than channel their philanthropy through conventional museums. There are now 317 private art museums (with active, living collector–founders) globally, but 70 per cent of them were built after 2000, and many of them work closely with artists that they collect (Larry's List/AMMA, 2016) and many, if not all of them, are radicalised by the art they collect. In the last 20 years a new group of artists have sought out relationships with eye-catching private collector museums once it was established that public art museums were increasingly unable to buy and give their works the public exposure they looked for (Franklin 2020).

At the other end of the spectrum, we saw a potential source of new, smaller, leaner, anti-museums in the inspiring model established by Art42 and especially the way it has been used to train the next generation of the Parisian art world.

Champions of other artists

The anti-museums considered here have also successfully championed artists who were unrecognised, ignored or without patronage. The Collection de l'Art Brut became the wellspring for a global efflorescence of recognition and support for mentally disabled and other socially isolated artists. James Brett's London-based Museum of Everything has extended the more restricted range of outsider artists to include others: the 'unintentional, untrained and undiscovered' artists everywhere. It is now vying, somewhat uncomfortably in the same market as contemporary art, as is the street art collected by Art42.

Equally, the New Museum was a conduit for women and ethnic minority artists in the 1980s and beyond, not only exhibiting their work systematically but supporting their art practices and causes. PS1 did much to identify and support installation artists and contemporary sculptors at a time when they too were struggling to find exhibitionary space and gallery support. Many of the major names, now celebrity artists, were supported at crucial stages by PS1 and the New Museum. The Chinati Foundation in Marfa offers a continuous stream of internships for artists as well as a means of supporting their practice and was the base from which the entire town has become an arts centre unlike any other. Even by 1987, Judd could claim his combined platform at Marfa as the 'the largest visible installations of contemporary art in the world', and it is still expanding, still inspiring others to build there on a similar scale using existing or derelict sites and buildings (Stockebrand 2010, p. 35). Likewise, through the 1990s and 2000s, Nicolas Laugero Lassere did much to support the art practice of street artists internationally, setting up new ways to extend their reach beyond the major cities, build careers and exhibitionary pathways and new sources of income. Whereas many conventional museums are extremely costly to make additions to, the low-cost basis of many anti-museum extensions are not and they can take advantage of spaces other than new buildings such as public spaces, natural areas, churches, disused hospital buildings and asylums, schools, unused industrial and port precincts, cinemas, supermarkets and markets. The demise of contemporary high streets is already offering a new generation of 'meanwhile spaces', unlettable stores and other favourable locations for artists, museums and galleries (Moorhead 2009; Youngs 2013; Eademariam 2019).

As an artefact of activism, as much as collecting or curation, anti-museums also find themselves being distributed into the fabric of political and social movement spaces and activities. Mona has become involved in the environmental politics of its locality and the New Museum has become involved in city activism, anti-gentrification, pro-diversity and housing and community issues within its own neighbourhood around its location on the Bowery/Soho. It has been highly sensitive to its own impact as a major arts institution, making sure that it has not been a stalking horse for developers, and seeking to strengthen the voices and presence of other members of its local community.

As an extension of the museum, Mona co-produced (with the City of Hobart and the State of Tasmania) two important music and arts festivals at midsummer and midwinter. The latter, Dark Mofo, has become very significant to its tourism and cultural communities (McGarry 2018; Franklin 2020). In Dark Park, one of the industrial spaces it activated during Dark Mofo, it has now set up Dark Lab, an urban design-cum-think tank wing of its collaborations with the State Government and City of Hobart in order to plan a major new urban development at the Macquarie Point waterfront where art can thrive alongside urban expansion.

Places on the margin (anti-structure)

The anti-museums considered here are, in one or more respects, in out-of-the-way places, or more precisely, places on the *social* margin. While

Art42 is still in Paris, the 17th Arrondissement is a social world away from the 1st Arrondissement arts precinct. Equally, PS1 and New Museum's various addresses in New York have been far from the cultural epicentre and even today they still occupy interstitial spaces of the city. Mona and Marfa were once wild frontiers far away from civilisation, and in many respects, they are still remote areas requiring a very determined traveller to visit them. Lausanne sits on the edge of Lake Geneva, under high alpine country and is a long way off the cultural trails of Europe.

The act of travelling to these museum locations, arriving at them and spending time in them involves an experience of separation from the cultural centre and the everyday, together with a heightened emotional connection to their art. For these reasons, arriving at them feels more like a ritual occasion and one's time there is immersive and transformational. One has more time for art than is normally the case, and time seems to take on a different rhythm and meaning.

Ideally art is supposed to be transformational, to possess the capacity to change us, though it often eludes those who looks for it, or look too hard for it in the wrong places. All of the art I encountered in these anti-museums seemed to have a special quality; it was *lively* in that there was an active purpose behind its assembly in ways that connect it to ongoing relations with the world beyond its walls and to us, the viewers. It does not take much to feel the agency of this art and through it, to the network of connections it has assembled.

Trusting the intelligence of visitors

During visits to these anti-museums, it became clear that none of them were interested in didacticism. They did not wish to instruct, set themselves up as an authority or act as an arbiter of taste. Labelling is rather rare and/or minimal and there is very little attempt to direct or shape a museum experience. To use one of Mona's stock phrases, 'they show, they do not tell'. To do this requires a great deal of restraint as well as a great deal of *trust*. But in all cases considered here, the minimisation of labels, instruction and direction appears to produce more rather than less engagement. In the case of Mona there is solid evidence to demonstrate that there is considerably less museum fatigue. This was observed in all of the institutions featured in this book, though that remains to be formally verified in every case.

David Walsh, like Donald Judd before him, trusted his visitors to have sufficient intelligence to form an engagement of some kind with their art. Both believed it important to leave visitors alone with art and not to mediate their gaze. Building a personal dialogue with artworks is a major step in building a connection:

> What is striking is that the art [at Mona] – its difficult, multiple meanings, its unpredictable effects and affects – is taken deadly seriously. Democratic access is not achieved by making it look like a department store or a bad version of Disneyland. Instead its success is in the belief that everybody can have a response to art at the deepest level – should they want to. It does not lack pedagogy but condescension. This is Mona's risk-taking – the belief that the public is made up of grown-ups. It is this, not the money or the glamour, which lies at the heart of its success.
>
> (O'Connor 2013)

Trust in the knowledgeability and value of 'non-expert' responses to art extends to those working in anti-museums. For example, visitor engagement at Art42 is organised and guided by students and Mona has non-expert opinion built into voices of communication (those of its writers, creative director and collector) and not all of its curators are professionally/conventionally trained. Most recently, its 2019 winter festival, Dark Mofo, featured the dystopian work *Aftermath Dislocation Principle* by Jimmy Cauty (of KLF fame) where children were given custody of the site and enrolled to navigate the work and offer their interpretation to viewers. The 1/30 scale model of the aftermath of a riot in small town Britain, assembled inside a large shipping container, was parked outside Hobart's Town Hall. As it toured 35 sites in the UK, Cauty realised that children, 'custodians of the future', were the 'best placed to communicate the ideas in the work' (Francis 2019).

Future research on the anti-museum

While few people would argue that the anti-museum should supersede the great anthology museums of the world, this book has argued that the anti-museums have added considerable value by extending the range of work that art museums can do, as well as contributing to museum pedagogy. However, there is only so much that a book of this kind can do to identify and test such claims. While this book has illustrated the great range and scope of museums that opt out of, or oppose strongly the more conventional models, it has also found a sufficient core of commonalities to justify more research. To date, scholarship in this area has been sparse, which is why so much of this volume has been documentary in nature. Given that museums of contemporary art are currently being built with great enthusiasm, many of them by private collectors, artists and public-facing if not publicly funded institutions such as fashion houses, corporations, independent research institutions (such as Wellcome Trust) and other not-for-profit organisations, and many of them are guided by less conventional aims, this research field is likely to grow. We have also hinted, at various points in the book, that some anti-museum advances and innovations have been embraced and taken into some of the more conventional museums, often to accommodate the particular needs of contemporary art. This was clearly the case when MoMa acquired PS1 to form MoMa PS1. The Tasmanian Museum and Art Gallery had a makeover in the likeness of Mona very soon after Mona opened. Will this process neutralise their interventions or distribute then more widely?

Hence it is important to conclude this book with a call for more research on these important museological experimenters and innovators, especially now when we are looking at an expansion of this field and a new willingness for risk, cooperation and convergence (Smith 2012). Such a view is not confined to those who position themselves outside the realm of conventional public art museums. It is instructive, for example, that major institutions such as the Museo Reina Sophia in Madrid are now beginning to write very different kinds of mission statements that align more with the cut and thrust of anti-museum thinking. In their opening statement, for example, they argue that:

> If the economic paradigm based on speculation and easy money has proven unsustainable, it should also be clear that the primacy of the building and of art as spectacle over the museum's artistic program has ceased to be valid. There is therefore a pressing need to invent other models.
>
> (Museo Reina Sophia, 2019)

References

Adorno, T 1999, *Aesthetic theory* (trans. R. Hullot-Kentor), Athlone Press, London.

Baker, J 2012, 'Darkness and affectivity: impressions of MONA (Museum of Old and New Art)', Cultural Heritage Centre for Asia and the Pacific Seminar Series, Deakin University. https://podcasts.apple.com/us/podcast/cultural-heritage-centre-for-asia-pacific-seminar-series/id550381689?l=de

Baker, J 2013, 'Out of the wilderness (MONA): critically engaging with the profound art encounter', in Grossman, GU and Krutisch, P (ed.), 33rd Congress of the International Committee of the History of Art, July 15–20 2012. Nuremberg: Verlag des Germanischen Nationalmuseums.

Barush, KR 2016, *Art and the sacred journey in Britain*, Routledge, London.

Bakhtin, M 1984, *Rabelais and his world*, University of Minnesota Press, Minneapolis.

Bastable, J 2010, 'The wheeler dealer', *Wallpaper*, December, p. 100.

Battaglia, A 2017, 'Alanna Heiss and Massimiliano Gioni in conversation', *The ARTnews Accord*, 5 February.

Benedetti, L 2019, 'Johannes Cladders' anti-museum. The exhibition as a platform for the new museum', *Cura Magazine*, https://curamagazine.com/cura-22-johannes-cladders-anti-museum-the-exhibition-as-a-platform-for-the-new-museum/

Benjamin, W 1955, 'Unpacking my library: a talk about book collecting', in H Arendt (ed.), *Illuminations: essays and reflections*, Brace and World, New York, pp. 59–67.

Bennett, T 1988, 'The exhibitionary complex', *New Formations*, vol. 4, Spring, pp. 73–102.

Bennett, T 1995, *The birth of the museum*, Routledge, Abingdon.

Berger, J 2018, *Landscapes*, Verso, London.

Bigot, R, Daudey, E, Hoibian, S & Müller, J 2013, *La visite des musées, des expositions et des monuments*, CREDOC, Paris.

Brewer, J 1979, 'Theater and counter-theater in Georgian politics: the mock elections at Garrat', *Radical History Review*, vol. 22, Winter, pp. 7–40.

Bristol, MD 1983, 'Carnival and the institutions of theater in Elizabethan England', *ELH*, vol. 50, no. 4, pp. 637–665.

Bruner, ML 2005, 'Carnivalesque protest and the humorless state,' *Text and Performance Quarterly*, vol. 25, no. 2, pp. 136–155.

Butler, B 2016, *Return to Alexandria: an ethnography of cultural heritage revivalism and museum memory*, Routledge, London.

Capon, E (dir.) 2013, *The art of Australia. A three-part TV documentary*, ABC, Sydney.

Cardinal, R 2000, 'The self in self-taught art', in C Russell (ed.), *Self-taught art: the culture and aesthetics of American vernacular art*, University of Mississippi, Mississippi, pp. 68–80.

Cladders, J 1968, '"The Antimuseum": artworks of the second half of the 20th century owned by the city of Mönchengladbach', exhibition catalog, Municipal Museum, Mönchengladbach.

Cleary, T 2006, *The New Museum: function, form and politics*, doctoral thesis, Griffith University.

Clocktower 2014, *Clocktower history*, viewed 27 October 2014, http://clocktower.org/about

Collings, M 2001, *Art crazy nation*, 21Publishing, London.

Collings, M 2003, *Sarah Lucas*, Tate, London.

Collinson, P 2016, 'Merry England on the ropes: the contested nature of the early modern English town', in S Ditchfield (ed.), *Christianity and community in the west*, Routledge, Oxon, pp. 131–47.

Connelly, F (ed.) 2003, *Modern art and the grotesque*, Cambridge University Press, Cambridge.

Copeland, M & Balthazar, L 2017, *The anti-museum: an anthology*, Koenig Books, Berlin.

Corwyn, W 2018, 'Nathaniel Mellors: progressive rocks', *The Brooklyn Rail*, 18 March.

Cranfield, B 2008, 'Introduction', *How soon is now: 60 years of the Institute of Contemporary Arts* [editor, Ekow Eshun, co-editor Pamela Jahn; contributing editor Martha Pym] Institute of Contemporary Art, London.

Cranfield, B 2014, 'All play and no work? a "ludistory" of the curatorial as transitional object at the early ICA', *Tate Papers*, no. 22, Autumn, www.tate.org.uk/research/publications/tate-papers/22/all-play-and-no-work-a-ludistory-of-the-curatorial-as-transitional-object-at-the-early-ica

Croome, R 2011, 'Mona: Croome, Marr, Cica, Allen, Denholm', *Tasmanian Times*, 31 December 2011.

Cross, R 1996, 'A guide to the Grand Canyon', *Chicago Tribune*, 27 October. www.chicagotribune.com/travel/chi-981213onpgrandcanyonguide-story.html

Cross, D 2006, *Some kind of beautiful: the grotesque body in contemporary art*, Doctoral thesis, Queensland University of Technology, Brisbane.

Daunton, MJ 1983, *House and home in a Victorian city*, Edward Arnold, London.

Davey, G 2005, 'What is museum fatigue?' *Visitor Studies Today*, vol. 8, no. 3, pp. 17–21.

Dubuffet, J 1949, 'L'art brut préféré aux arts culturels' in *L'Art Brut*, Collection de l'Art Brut, Lausanne.

Duncan, C & Wallach, A 1978, 'The museum of modern art as a late capitalist ritual', *Marxist Perspectives*, vol. 1, Winter, pp. 28–51.

Elkins, J 2010, 'How long does it take to look at a painting?' *Huffington Post*. 11 August, www.huffpost.com/entry/how-long-does-it-take-to_b_779946.

Fine, GA 2003, 'Crafting authenticity: the validation of identity in self-taught art', *Theory and Society*, vol. 32, pp. 153–180.

Flanagan, R 2013, 'Tasmanian Devil', *New Yorker Magazine*, vol. 88, no. 21, pp. 50–57.

Fol, C 2015, *From art brut to art without boundaries*, Skira, Milan.

Fones, R 1996, 'Amazing space: Donald Judd's works in Marfa', *C Magazine*, vol. 50, pp. 28–39.

Foster, H 2015, *Bad new days: art, criticism, emergency*, Verso, New York.

Francis, H 2019, 'Creepy much? The weirdest things at Dark Mofo 2019', *Sydney Morning Herald*, 15 June.

Franklin, AS 2014, *The making of Mona*, Penguin Books, Melbourne and London.

Franklin, AS 2018, 'The art of spreading the benefit', *The Mercury*, July 9, pp. 5–6.

Franklin, AS 2019, 'Where "art meets life": assessing the impact of Dark Mofo, a new mid-winter festival in Australia', *Journal of Festive Studies*, vol. 1, no. 1, Spring, pp. 106–127.

Franklin, AS 2020 (forthcoming), 'Mona and the political-cultural economy of independent galleries', in D Stevenson, T Bennett, F Myers & F Winikoff (eds), *The Australian art field: frictions and futures*, Melbourne University Press, Melbourne.

Franklin, AS & Papastergiadis, N 2017, 'Engaging with the anti-museum? Visitors to the Museum of Old and New Art (Mona)', *Journal of Sociology*, vol. 53, no. 3, pp. 670–686.

Franklin, AS & Sansom, M 2018, '"Aimless and absurd wanderings"? children at the Museum of Old and New Art (Mona)', *Museum and Society*, vol. 16, no. 1, pp. 28–40.

Fraser, A 2005, 'From the critique of institutions to an institution of critique', *Artforum*, vol. 44, no. 1, pp. 278–286.

Fraser, M 2013, 'Introduction and explanatory notes to MONA archive 2007', personal communication to the author from Mark Fraser, Mona Museum Director 2007–2011

Ganning, JP 2016, 'Arts stability and growth amid redevelopment in U.S. shrinking cities' downtowns', *Economic Development Quarterly*, vol. 30, no. 3, pp. 239–251.

Giebelhausen, M 2003, *The architecture of the museum: symbolic structures, urban contexts*, MUP, Manchester.

Gladstone, M 2012, 'Marcia Tucker and the birth of the New Museum', *Getty Research Journal*, vol. 4, pp. 187–194.

Goldberg, R 1980, 'Performance – art for all'? *Art Journal*, vol. 40, no. 1/2, Modernism, Revisionism, Plurism, and Post-Modernism (Autumn–Winter, 1980), pp. 369–376

Gnyp, M 2015, *The shift: art and the rise to power of contemporary collectors*, Art and Theory Publishing, Stockholm.

Green, A 2018, *Where artists curate – contemporary art and the exhibition as medium*, Reaktion, London.

Grima, J 2017, 'Ideas city: the museum as platform for civic action', in L Phillips (ed.), *New museum*, New Museum/Phaidon, New York.

Gzeley, N 2017, *Roman Froquet: entre les lignes*, Criteres Editions, Grenoble.

Hanquinet, L & Savage, M 2012, 'Educative leisure and the art museum', *Museum and Society*, vol. 10, no. 1, pp. 42–59.

Heckmüller, S 2011, *Privatzugang: private kunstsammlungen in Deutschland, Österreich und der Schweiz*, Distanz, Berlin.

Heiss, A 2012, *Placing the artist: 100 notes – 100 thoughts, No. 074*, Kassell, Germany.

Hill, P 2011, 'The culture chthonic and iconic', *Times Higher Education*, 24 February, pp. 47–48.

Housen, A 1987, 'Three methods for understanding museum audiences', *Museum Studies Journal*, vol. 2, Summer/Spring, pp. 41–49.

Huyssen, A 1986, *After the great divide: modernism, mass culture and postmodernism*, Macmillan, London.

Ikin, S 2015, 'Lonely Planet names three Tasmanian destinations in "Ultimate Travelist"', ABC News, 18 August, www.abc.net.au/news/2015-08-18/lonely-planet-names-three-tas-destinations-in-ultimate-travelist/67042785-6

Iniesta, V 2016, *Art 42*, Criteres Editions, Grenoble.

Jervis, J 1999, *Transgressing the modern*, Blackwell, Oxford.

Judd, D 1973, 'Complaints: Part II', *Arts Magazine*, March 1973.

Judd, D 2016, *Donald Judd writings*, Judd Foundation/David Zwirner Books, New York.

Kellein, T, 2010, 'Foreword', in Stockebrand, M, *Chinati: the vision of Donald Judd*, Marfa Foundation in association with Yale University Press, Marfa.

Kennedy, R 2017, 'The most powerful woman in the New York art world', *New York Times*, viewed 29 May 2019, www.nytimes.com/2017/05/04/arts/design/new-museum-director-lisa-phillips.html

Kimmelman, M 2001, *New York Times*, 4 February, www.nytimes.com/2001/02/04/arts/art-architecture-the-last-great-art-of-the-20th-century.html

Krauss, R 1990, 'The cultural logic of late capitalist museums', *October* 54 (Fall 1 1990), pp. 3–17.

Kundera, M 2006, *The art of the novel*, Faber, London.

Laird, M 2018, 'Art brut joins the market frenzy', *Swiss Info*, viewed 29 May 2019, www.swissinfo.ch/eng/from-outsider-to-mainstream_art-brut-joins-the-market-frenzy/37714722

Lang, R 2017, 'A tour through the best museums in Australia', SBS Radio, 18 May.

Leahy, HR 2010, 'Watch your step: embodiment and encounter at the Tate Modern', in S Dudley (ed.), *Museum materialities: objects, engagements, interpretations*, Routledge, London, pp. 162–174.

Lerner, N 1987, *Henry Darger: artists protector of children*, adapted from a taped interview by J MacGregor, included as a 'Foreword' in MacGregor 2002.

Ley, D 2003, 'Artists, aestheticisation and the field of gentrification', *Urban Studies*, vol. 40, no. 12, pp. 2527–2544.

Lombardi, S 2018, *Art brut: from Japan, another look*, Collection de l'Art Brut, Lausanne.

Lonely Planet 2013, www.lonelyplanet.com/themes/best-in-travel/top-10-cities/#ixzz42ITWa9qF

Lorente, JP 2011, *The museums of contemporary art*, Ashgate, Farnham.

Lorente, JP 2016, 'From the white cube to a critical museography: the development of interrogative, plural and subjective museum discourses', in KM Muthesius & P Piotrowski (eds), *From museum critique to the critical museum*, Routledge, London, pp. 131–144.

Louie, E 1997, 'The new P.S. 1: contemporary art, but the building's the star', *New York Times*, 2 October.

Maak, N, Klonk, C & Demand, T 2011 'The white cube and beyond', *Museum Display, Tate Etc.*, Issue 21, spring 2011.

Macdonald, S 2008, 'Museum Europe. Negotiating heritage', *Anthropological Journal of European Cultures,* vol. 17, pp. 47–65.

MacGregor, JM 2002, *The Vivian girls*, trans. K Koide, Sakuhinsya & Co, Tokyo.

Maclagan, D 2010, *Outsider art: from the margins to the marketplace*. Reaktion: London.

Maizels, J (ed.) 2016, *Outsider art sourcebook*, Raw Vision, Watford.

Maleuvre, D 1999, *Museum memories*, Stanford University Press, Stanford.

Marinetti, FT 1909, 'The founding and manifesto of futurism', in L Cahoone (ed.), *From modernism to postmodernism: an anthology*, Blackwell Publishers, Oxford, pp. 118–121.

Marr, D 2008, *The Henson case*, Text Publishing, Melbourne.

Marshall, C 2016, *Baroque Naples and the industry of painting: the world in the workbench*, Yale University Press, New Haven.

Martin, JH, *Theatre of the world*, exhibition catalogue, 23 June 2012–8 April 2013, Mona, Hobart.

Matthews, V 2010, 'Aestheticizing space: art, gentrification and the city,' *Geography Compass*, vol. 4, no. 6, pp. 660–675.

Matthews, V 2014, 'Incoherence and tension in culture-led redevelopment', *International Journal of Urban and Regional Research*, vol. 38, no. 3, pp. 1019–1036.

McCarthy, B 2018, *Destination art*. Phaidon, London.

McClellan, A 2008, *The art museum: from Boullee to Bilbao*, California University Press, Berkeley.

McGarry, M 2018, The Mona effect: regeneration in the dark, doctoral thesis, University of Tasmania, Tasmania.

McKay, G and Webster, E 2016, 'From Glyndebourne to Glastonbury: the impact of British music festivals', Arts and Humanities Research Council/University of East Anglia, Norwich.

Merrick, J 2010, 'Brut force: the Lille Art Museum extension', *Independent*, 26 September.

Miller, D 2008, *The comfort of things*, Polity, Cambridge.

Miller, MH 2016, 'The anti-museum director: Alanna Heiss on the 40th anniversary of PS1 contemporary art center', *Artnews*, Spring.

Mintern, KM 2007, Contre-Histoire: the postwar art and writings of Jean Dubuffet, doctoral thesis, Columbia University, Columbia.

Morenne, B 2016, 'Street art heads to the museum in France', *New York Times*, 28 October.

Museo Reina Sophia 2019, 'Mission statement', viewed 29 May 2019, www.museoreinasofia.es/en/museum/mission-statement

Museum of Everything 2011, *You're not only human*, Museum of Everything, London.

National Endowment for the Arts, 2019, www.arts.gov/file/226. Sourced 29 June 2019.

Nelson, M 2018, 'No excuses', in New Museum (ed.), *Sarah Lucas Au Naturel*, New Museum/Phaidon, New York.

O'Connor, J 1999, *Cultural production in Manchester: mapping and strategy*, Institute for Popular Culture, Manchester Metropolitan University, Manchester, www.mmu.ac.uk/h-ss/mipc/iciss.

O'Connor, J 2010, *The cultural and creative industries: a literature review*, Creativity, Culture and Education, Newcastle.

O'Connor, J 2013, 'David Walsh's Mona and the cultural regeneration of Hobart', *The Conversation*, viewed 29 May 2019, https://theconversation.com/david-walshsmona-and-the-cultural-regeneration-of-hobart-15718

Parris, M 2011, 'My Tasmanian rhapsody', *The Times*, viewed 29 May 2019, www.thetimes.co.uk/article/my-tasmanian-rhapsody-kj8fnclwqx9

Peiry, L 2001, *Art brut: the origins of outsider art*, trans. J Frank, Flammarion, Paris.

Phillips, L 2017, *New museum*, New Museum/Phaidon, New York.

Phillips, L, Burton, B, Ritson, A & Wiener, K 2019, *Out of bounds: the collected writings of Marcia Tucker*, Getty Research Institute, New York.

Piper, A 1983, *Funk lessons*, videotape, University of California, Berkeley.

Prior, N 2002, *Museums and modernity: art galleries and the making of modern culture*, Berg, Oxford.

Radywyl, N, Papastergiadis, N, Douglas, A & Mcquire, S 2011, 'Ambient aesthetics: altered subjectivities in the new museum', in K Message & S MacDonald (eds), *Museum theory: an expanded field*, Blackwell, Oxford, pp. 417–436.

Reid, D 1982, 'Interpreting the festival calendar: wakes and fairs as carnivals', in RD Storch (ed.), *Popular culture and custom in nineteenth-century England*, St. Martin's Press, New York, pp. 125–153.

Rentschler, R 2015, *Arts governance: people, passion, performance*, Routledge, London.

Rich, AM & Tsitsos, W 2016, 'Avoiding the "SoHo effect" in Baltimore: neighborhood revitalization and arts and entertainment districts', *International Journal of Urban and Regional Research*, vol. 40, no. 4, pp. 736–756.

Rifkin, N 2017, 'Alternative geographies: art in New York and beyond', in L Phillips (ed.), *New museum*, New Museum/Phaidon, New York.

Ritchie, B 2011, 'Brian Ritchie on Mona Foma', *Perspectives*, Arts Northern Rivers, Lismore, NSW.

Roberts, J 1997, 'The crisis of critical postmodernism' in AW Balkema & H Slager *The photographic paradigm. Vol 12 of Lier and Boog: series of philosophy of art and art theory*, Rodopi, Amsterdam, pp. 67–74.

Roberts J 2015, *Revolutionary time and the avant-garde*, Verso, London.

Rorty, R 1989, *Contingency, irony and solidarity*, Cambridge University Press, Cambridge.

Roud, S 2008, *The English year*, Penguin, Harmondsworth.

Rousseau, V 2010, 'Révéler l'Art Brut: À La Recherche D'un Musée', *Culture & Musées*, vol. 16, no. 1, pp. 65–92.

Rousseau, V 2018, 'At the beginning, a monologue: the fate of self-taught art', *The Brooklyn Rail – Critical Perspectives on Art, Politics and Culture*, 18 July.

Ruiz, C 2010, 'A "subversive Disneyland" at the end of the world', *Art Newspaper*, no. 215, July, pp. 30–31.

Ryzik, M 2015, 'The guerrilla girls, after 3 decades, still rattling art world cages', *New York Times*, 5 August. www.nytimes.com/2015/08/09/arts/design/the-guerrilla-girls-after-3-decades-still-rattling-art-world-cages.html. Sourced 4 July 2019.

Sachs Olsen, C 2019, *Socially engaged art and the neoliberal city*, Routledge, London.

Sasajima, H 2016, 'Artist-led gentrification of SoHo in New York City', *Japanese Sociological Review*, vol. 67, no. 1, pp. 65–80.

Saumarez Smith, C 1995, 'Architecture and the museum: the seventh Reyner Banham memorial lecture', *Journal of Design History*, vol. 8, no. 4, pp. 243–256.

Schuetz, J 2014, 'Do art galleries stimulate redevelopment?', *Journal of Urban Economics*, vol. 83, no. 59, pp. 59–72.

Serota, N 2000, *Experience or interpretation: the dilemma of museums of modern art*. Thames & Hudson, London.

Serota, N 2004, 'Journey into space', *Guardian*, 17 January.

Serrell, B 1997, 'Paying attention: the duration and allocation of visitors' time in museum exhibitions', *Curator*, vol. 40, no. 2, pp. 108–125.

Shafer, K 2017, *Marfa: the transformation of a West Texan town*, University of Texas Press, Austin.

Shaw, K & Porter, L 2009, 'Introduction', in L Porter & K Shaw (eds), *Whose urban renaissance*, Routledge, London, pp. 1–19.

Sherman, D 1994, 'Quatremere/Benjamin/Marx: art museums, aura, and commodity fetishism', in D Sherman & I Rogoff (eds), *Museum culture, histories, discourses, spectacles*, University of Minnesota Press, Minneapolis, pp. 123–143.

Shields, FA 2007, The transubstantiation of Henry Darger, doctoral thesis, University of British Columbia, British Columbia.

Simpson, P 2015, 'The history of street performance: "music by handle" and the silencing of street musicians in the metropolis', *Gresham College*, viewed 29 May 2019, www.gresham.ac.uk/lectures-and-events/the-history-of-street-performance

Smith, R 1994, 'Donald Judd, leading minimalist sculptor, dies at 65', *New York Times*, 13 February.

Smith, T 2009, *What is contemporary art?* University of Chicago Press, Chicago.

Smith, T 2012, *Thinking contemporary curating*, Independent Curators International, New York.

Snell, T 2017, 'The compulsion to create: "outsider art" at MONA's The Museum of Everything', *The Conversation*, 14 June, http://theconversation.com/the-compulsion-to-create-outsider-art-at-monas-the-museum-of-everything-79329

Sortiraparis 2019, 'Fluctuart, the world's first floating urban art center in Paris, this spring'. www.sortiraparis.com/news/in-paris/articles/147392-fluctuart-the-worlds-first-floating-urban-art-center-in-paris-this-spring-2019/lang/en)#GwfX1oDsHLAL5lrr.99. Sourced 1 June 2019.

Stallybrass, J 2006, *High art lite*, Verso, London.

Stockebrand, M 2010, *Chinati: the vision of Donald Judd*, Marfa Foundation in association with Yale University Press, Marfa.

Storch, RD (ed.) 1982, *Popular culture and custom in nineteenth-Century England*, St Martin's Press, New York.

Schweizer Tourismus-Verband 2017, *Swiss tourism in figures 2017*, www.stv-fst.ch/sites/default/files/2018-07/stiz_en.pdf

Thévoz, M 1985, *Art, folie, graffiti, LSD etc.* L'Aire, Lausanne.

Thévoz, M 1991, *Letter to the Director of the Centre Regional de Formation des Maitres de Besancon*, letter, Lausanne Archives, Lausanne.

Thévoz, M 1993, *Michel Thévoz interviewed by Esther Gondalez Martinez, Lausanne*, Lausanne Archives, Lausanne.

Thévoz, M 1994, 'An anti-museum,' in MD Hall & EW Metcalf Jr (eds), *The artist outsider: creativity and the boundaries of culture*, Smithsonian Institution Press, Washington, pp. 62–75.

Thévoz, M 1995, *Requiem pour la folie*, La Difference, Paris.

Thévoz, M 2001, 'The strange hell of beauty ….', in CG Sweeney (ed.), *Darger: the Henry Darger collection at the American Folk Art Museum*, Harry N. Abrams Inc, New York, pp. 15–21.

Thévoz, Michel 1975, *L'art brut*, Albert Skira, Genève.

Thompson, EP 1992, 'Rough music revisited', *Folklore*, vol. 102, no. 1, pp. 3–26.

Tillman, L 2017, 'Early years of the new museum: an intellectual reminiscence or pieces from a consciousness', in L Phillips (ed.), *New museum*, New Museum/Phaidon, New York, pp. 81–88.

Timms, P 2011a, 'Mona reframes the game,' *The Age*, 28 May.

Timms, P 2011b, '"A post-Google wonderkammer": museum of old and new art redefines the genre', *Meanjin Quarterly*, vol. 70, no. 2, https://meanjin.com.au/essays/a-postgoogle-wunderkammer-hobarts-museum-of-old-and-new-art-redefines-the-genre/

Urbaschek, S 2003, *Dia Art Foundation Institution und Sammlung 1974–1985*, Tectum, Verlag Marberg.

Verghis, S 2016, 'MONA's on the origin of art: David Walsh's tale of four visions', *The Australian*, 22 October.

Wallis, B 2017, 'The museum as site: art and activism at the new museum', in L Phillips (ed.), *New museum*, New Museum/Phaidon, New York.

Webb, D 2005, 'Bakhtin at the seaside: utopia, modernity and the carnivalesque', *Theory, Culture & Society*, vol. 22, no. 3, pp. 121–138.

Witcomb, A 2003, *Re-imagining the museum: beyond the mausoleum*, Routledge, London.

Wilsey, S & Beal, D 2012, 'Lone star bohemia', *Vanity Fair*, July 2012.
Yarinsky, A 2011, 'Donald Judd and the blooming of reality: the art and architecture of Donald Judd, from Soho to Marfa', *Places Journal*, viewed 29 May 2019, https://placesjournal.org/article/donald-judd-and-the-blooming-of-reality/?cn-reloaded=1\
Youngs, I 2013, 'The creative boom in empty buildings', BBC News November 13, www.bbc.com/news/entertainment-arts-24871292
Zukin, S 1995, *The culture of cities*, Blackwell, Oxford.
Zukin, S 2010, *Naked city*, Blackwell, Oxford.

Index

Page numbers in **bold** denote tables, those in *italics* denote figures.

For Product Safety Concerns and Information please contact our EU representative GPSR@taylorandfrancis.com
Taylor & Francis Verlag GmbH, Kaufingerstraße 24, 80331 München, Germany

www.ingramcontent.com/pod-product-compliance
Lightning Source LLC
LaVergne TN
LVHW010922110826
845149LV00013B/2443